The Revolutionary War

The
MILITARY HISTORY
of the
UNITED STATES

Christopher Chant

THE REVOLUTIONARY WAR

MARSHALL CAVENDISH
NEW YORK · LONDON · TORONTO · SYDNEY

Library Edition Published 1992

© Marshall Cavendish Limited 1992

Published by
Marshall Cavendish Corporation
2415 Jerusalem Avenue
PO Box 587
North Bellmore
New York 11710

Series created by Graham Beehag Book Design

Series Editor	Maggi McCormick
Consultant Editors	James R. Arnold
	Roberta Wiener
Sub Editor	Julie Cairns
Designer	Graham Beehag
Illustrators	John Batchelor
	Steve Lucas
	Terry Forest
	Colette Brownrigg
Indexer	Mark Dartford

Library of Congress Cataloging-in-Publication Data

Chant, Christopher.
    The Military History of the United States / Christopher Chant –
Library ed.
        p. cm.
    Includes bibliographical references and index.
    Summary: Surveys the wars that have directly influenced the
United States., from the Revolutionary War through the Cold War.
    ISBN 1-85435-352-7 ISBN 1-85435-361-9 (set)
    1. United States - History, Military - Juvenile literature.
    |1. United States - History, Military.| I. Title.
    t181.C52 1991
    973 - dc20   90 - 19547
                                                              CIP
                                                               AC

Printed in Singapore by Times Offset PTE Ltd
Bound in the United States

The publishers wish to thank the following organizations
who have supplied photographs:

The National Archives, Washington. United States
Navy, United States Marines, United States Army,
United States Air Force, Department of Defense,
Library of Congress, The Smithsonian Institution.

The publishers gratefully thank the following organizations for the use of archive material for the following
witness accounts:

Page 18
U.S. Army Military History Institute, Carlisle Barracks,
PA. From the Revolutionary War Miscellaneous
Collection – Letter , August 13, 1775, Robert Magaw,
Thompson's Rifle Regiment. Also from *The British
Invasion from the North. The Campaigns of Generals
Carlton and Burgoyne from Canada 1776-1777, with
the journal of Liet. William Digby of the 53rd or
Shropshire regiment of foot*, by James Phinney
Baxter(Albany, 1887).

Pages 40-41
*Traditions and Reminiscencess Chiefly of the
American Revolution in the South* by Joseph Johnson,
M.D. (Charleston, 1853).

Pages 70-71
U.S. Army Military History Institute, Carlisle Barracks,
PA. *Memoir of John Stark* by Thomas Mullen
(Concord, 1877).

Pages 108-110
U.S. Army Military History Institute, Carlisle Barracks,
PA. The Sol Feinstone Collection of the American
Revolution.

Contents of Set

Contents of Set

Contents of Set

Contents of Set

Contents of Set

Contents of Set

Contents of Set

Readers Guide

Purpose

The purpose behind *The Military History of the United States* is to provide an objective work of reference on the wars, both great and small, fought by the American forces from 1776 to the present day. Many works about individual American wars and campaigns have been published, but the present work is specifically designed for school library use as an overview that also highlights the development of the American military within the context of the United States' steady emergence to world power. As such, *The Military History of the United States* deals not only with wars, but also with the evolution of the American military establishment and American military thinking through the entire period.

This introduction to *The Military History of the United States* is designed to provide the reader with a full description of what is to be found in the set, where it is, and how to find it.

Structure and Content

The Military History of the United States is a sixteen-volume set of fifteen volumes of narrative text and a sixteenth volume containing a complete index, a comprehensive glossary of technical terms, and a substantial bibliography.

Indexing

Each of the first fifteen volumes contains its own A-Z Index for quick reference within the volume, as well as cross-reference panels throughout the work to allow the user to find other references to major personalities and events. Volume 16 contains a fully comprehensive, cross-referenced A-Z Index to the whole set containing more than 8,000 entries.

Bibliography

There is an extensive English language bibliography of currently available publications in each volume, and Volume 16 contains a comprehensive bibliography of the whole work. A particular feature of the bibliographies is the supplementary annotation that provides the reader with a brief sketch of the content and scope of the books.

Front Matter

The contents of the entire set are listed in volume 1. Each volume also contains a contents list for that volume.

Text

The narrative text covers the major wars and minor conflicts involving the American forces since 1776, and the arrangement of the narrative is broadly chronological. The Civil War, World War II, and the Vietnam War are each covered in two volumes; single-volume coverage is used for the Revolutionary War, the Indian Wars, and World War I; and the smaller wars and campaigns are organized in the remaining volumes in chronological and/or geographical groupings.

Illustration

There are over 1,500 illustrations in *The Military History of the United States*, The bulk of the illustration is provided by contemporary photographs, engravings, and paintings, but important contributions are made by maps and colored drawings of uniforms and important weapons.

It is hoped that a working knowledge of the components of *The Military History of the United States* will enable the reader to make the fullest use of the set, enhancing its value as as a research tool, educational reference source, and general interest.

Contents of Volume

Origins of the War

The United States of America was created by the Revolutionary War out of 13 British colonies on the eastern seaboard of North America. The upheaval that followed the colonies' attempt to separate themselves from Great Britain was considerable, and during it modern history's first democratic republic came into being when the Declaration of Independence was signed on July 4, 1776. The Revolutionary War had already started in 1775, and its outcome was to force the British to recognize the existence of the new nation and give up its claims to the region.

Ironically, the American Revolution was caused by the final British triumph over the French for effective control of what is now the United States and Canada. As an outgrowth of the Seven Years' War, fought in Europe between 1756 and 1763, the French and Indian War started in 1754, ended in 1760, and was a decisive British victory that removed the French threat to the inhabitants of Great Britain's American colonies. The Treaty of Paris that formally ended the war in February 1763 also ceded the French possessions in Canada and in America east of the Mississippi River to the British, who created the far smaller British colony of Quebec along the St. Lawrence River.

Historical forces were already at work, pushing the colonies toward a separation from British rule. These forces gathered momentum at the end of the French and Indian War when the British, who were determined to strengthen their control in North America, announced that a per-

Paul Revere's engraving of the Boston Massacre was a clever and effective piece of propaganda for the American cause. In the real event on March 5, 1770, the British opened fire on a riotous mob of toughs, many of them armed with clubs and other weapons, who were pelting them with rocks and pieces of ice. Copied from a more detailed engraving by Henry Pelham, Revere's version of the event shows the British firing on a peaceful assembly of unarmed and defenseless Boston citizens.

The strength of American feeling against the British is revealed by an episode that took place in Boston on January 27, 1774, as a protest against the customs dues imposed by the British. Angry Americans stormed into the house of John Malcolm, a British revenue officer. Malcolm wounded several Americans with his sword, but was seized, lowered from a window, and then tarred and feathered.

manent force of 10,000 British troops was to be stationed on the American frontiers. The colonists were shocked by the additional news that the colonies themselves would have to pay a large part of the cost for a force they felt was not needed since the defeat of France and which was probably to be used for the suppression of American liberties. This was just one of several British tax moves that greatly angered Americans, who had for some time already called for "no taxation without representation" in the British parliament.

From 1763, colonial leaders urged the creation of American popular assemblies to levy taxes on Americans for American purposes, but the British constantly refused to allow the creation of such bodies.

The provisions of the Stamp Act and the

Sugar Act had already caused great resentment among the colonists. Between 1770 and 1774, there was growing violence and unrest, especially in the northern colonies. The British had felt themselves forced into repressive action in the so-called "Battle of Golden Hill" in New York during January 1770 and the "Boston Massacre" during March 1770. More serious trouble broke out on the western frontier of North Carolina during 1771, when a group of frontier settlers (self-styled "Regulators" mainly of Irish and Scottish descent) rose against the local aristocracy and called for intervention from London on their behalf. The governor sent in the colonial militia, which firmly defeated the Regulators in the Alamance Creek fight of May 16, 1771.

Among many British laws unpopular in the American colonies, the Stamp Act was perhaps the one that provoked the strongest feelings. In August 1775, American militants in Boston burned copies of the act's proclamation that had arrived from Great Britain.

The "Boston Tea Party"

The last straw for the British was the "Boston Tea Party" of December 16, 1773, when a group of Bostonians badly disguised as Indians, threw a consignment of British tea into the city's harbor to indicate their disgust with British taxation of the colonies. In the following year, the passage of the Quebec Act by the British parliament also alarmed the Americans. This new act expanded Quebec to the Ohio and Mississippi rivers, which was seen in the American colonies as a direct threat to the economic interests of Virginia and Pennsylvania.

Time was rapidly running out for the British to set matters right in their North American colonies. Colonial leaders had been trying since 1763 to persuade the British government to see the justice of

Boston
For further references
see pages
6, 7, 9, 10, 11, 17, 19,
27, 34, 38, 38, 43.

the colonists' points of view, and to convince the rulers that colonial hopes were both practical and not anti-British On two counts, the British made the wrong moves: on the one hand they failed to appreciate the revised and workable type of imperial union proposed by the colonists, and on the other, they also failed to act strongly enough to impose effective British rule on the colonies.

After the "Boston Tea Party," Parliament, with the full support of King George III, pushed through legislation that became known in the colonies as the "Intolerable Acts." These closed the port of Boston, infringed several of the colonists' rights and, to add insult to injury, imposed military rule on Massachusetts, which was now controlled directly by Major General Sir Thomas Gage. Gage was heavy-handed in his control of the colony, and this played into the hands of the American leaders, who had already raised colonial fears of increasingly repressive British rule. It is probable, therefore, that the declaration of martial rule in Massachusetts was the spark that ignited the tinder of the American Revolution.

The First Continental Congress Meets

On September 5, 1774, the First Continental Congress met in Philadelphia for a session that lasted until October 26 of the same year. The Congress drafted petitions to the king and Parliament in an effort to win repeal of the "Intolerable Acts." It also created a series of intercolonial agreements to prevent the import of British goods and the export of American ones to Great Britain, hoping in this way to exert financial pressure on the British. To make sure that these agreements were enforced, committees were formed in nearly every county, town, and city, and these committees soon became the real organs of government in the colonies. On this base, an organization of assemblies, congresses, conventions supervised by a few committees of safety

Another measure that infuriated the colonists was the British tax on the import of tea. On December 16, 1773, a group of protesters disguised as Indians boarded a British ship that had just arrived in Boston harbor and threw its cargo of tea into the sea. The British reacted by reducing the amount of self-government Massachusetts was allowed.

developed, although in greater secrecy. The British thus lost political control of the colonies at the grass-roots level. At the same time, this fledgling American government assumed control of the various militia forces, and thus paved the way for the creation of an American army.

The focus of activity in the short term was Massachusetts, and within Massachusetts the city of Boston. Here the Provincial Congress ordered that in each town one-third of the militia should be organized into "minuteman" units able to respond to a crisis at a moment's notice. To provide these forces with the required supplies, the Provincial Congress ordered the collection of ammunition and other stores at a depot in Concord, about 20 miles northwest of Boston.

Paul Revere's Ride

On April 18, 1775, Gage ordered a detachment of 700 British troops to march from Boston and seize the Concord depot. The plans were made in the greatest secrecy and the force marched off during the night, but the colonists had been expecting such a move. In a celebrated "midnight ride," Paul Revere, John Dawes, and Dr. Samuel Prescott rode ahead of the British force to warn the American patriots of the British move. Thus, when the British force marched into Lexington, slightly more than halfway from Boston to Concord, at dawn on April 19 they found that 70 American minutemen under Captain John Parker had taken up position on the village green. A

Above left: Depicted in its opening session in Philadelphia on September 5, 1774, the First Continental Congress marked the first genuinely "national" move by the American colonies. The congress urged the British to repeal the "Intolerable Acts," but also launched a series of agreements to limit British goods being imported into the 13 colonies.
Above: News of the Declaration of Independence is announced to the people of Boston.

gun was fired - and to this day it is not known whether it was an American or a British finger which pulled the trigger that fired this "shot heard 'round the world" - and the British regulars fired a volley into the minutemen before charging with their bayonets. The minutemen broke and dispersed, leaving eight of their men dead and another 10 wounded on Lexington Green.

The Revolutionary War had started. Major John Pitcairn pushed on with his British soldiers to Concord and found that the Americans had evacuated most of the supplies, burned the rest and set off back to Boston. By this time, the efforts of the "midnight riders" had raised the countryside into a hornet's nest of American minutemen and militia. The British force marched back toward Boston as fast as they could, but from

behind what seemed to be every rock, tree, and house, American fire poured out at them. By the time the force reached Charlestown, just north of Boston, with the aid of a relief column sent out to meet it, the British had lost 73 killed, 174 wounded, and 26 missing out of a total of 1,800 men. On the other side of the fence, almost literally, the Americans had suffered another 77 casualties to add to their 18 at Lexington.

In purely military terms, the Americans had not done as well as they might have hoped. During the course of the day they fired 75,000 rounds at the British and caused relatively few casualties. But more important by far was the boost in morale given to the revolution by the steadfast resistance of these New England citizens who had shown that no longer were Americans prepared to stand for British

Right: The most celebrated of the "midnight riders," Paul Revere raced through the Massachusetts countryside on the night of April 18-19, 1775, to warn patriots that the British were advancing on Concord.

Left: Contemporary illustrations liked to emphasize that the "minutemen" were ordinary farmers. Called by a "midnight rider," this minuteman sets off for battle, leaving behind his anguished mother, wife, and child.
Above left: The American colonies and the main battle sites of the Revolutionary War.
Above: The Battle of Lexington, where the American Revolution truly started.

domination through armed strength. Messengers rode throughout the 13 colonies as fast as exhausted horses could carry them, and within a short time, every colonist between New Hampshire and Georgia "knew" that the British had started a savage and unprovoked attack which had been repulsed by Massachusetts farmers, whose only thought had been to save their families and homes. It was a propaganda masterstroke, though probably not planned as such. Other colonial militia forces were called to arms, and offers of aid poured in to the Provincial Congress.

The Siege of Boston

In Boston, the Provincial Congress had decided to raise a force of 13,600 volunteers to besiege the British garrison of the city, and overall command of this Massachusetts force was entrusted to Major General Artemas Ward. Offers of aid from other colonies were gratefully accepted, and soon detachments were arriving from Connecticut, New Hampshire and Rhode Island so that the small British garrison was trapped by 15,000 Americans.

Below: The Battle of Concord before the British withdrawal to Boston.

Benedict Arnold was a key figure in the Revolutionary War. This capable military commander served the American cause well during the first stage of the war, but was then paid to "turn his coat" and support the British in the second.

The uprising was also spreading to other parts of the colonies. The two most notable episodes were the capture of Ticonderoga and Crown Point, British forts on Lakes George and Champlain that formed the best route by which British forces could march from Quebec into the Hudson River valley in order to move on New York and the New England colonies. Ticonderoga was taken by Connecticut militia under Colonel Benedict Arnold on May 10, 1775, while Crown Point was taken two days later by Vermont militia, the "Green Mountain Boys" under Colonel Ethan Allen, who had refused to accept a command under Arnold.

The capture of these two places helped to prevent the move of British reinforcements from Quebec and also provided the revolutionary forces with much useful equipment, including some artillery. On the other side of the coin, however, Allen's

Major General, British Army (1775-1781)

From 1767, British generals had two coats: one was a gold-laced type for state occasions, while the other was a plainer "frock" in scarlet with blue facings and some gold embroidery. This major general is seen with his coat buttoned across his chest in the manner considered fashionable at the time for generals in the field. The coats of lieutenant generals had their button holes set in triplets while those for major generals were set in pairs. There was no uniformity of epaulets, which were often not worn.

refusal to serve under Arnold is an early example of the problem that would often be faced by revolutionary leaders in uniting colonial forces under a single command.

Two days after the capture of Fort Ticonderoga, the Americans achieved success in the first "naval" action of the war. In Machias Bay, Maine (then a part of Massachusetts), a group of lumbermen under Jeremiah O'Brien captured the British armed cutter *Margaretta*.

On the day that Fort Ticonderoga fell, the Second Continental Congress assembled, again in Philadelphia. But while the First Continental Congress had been limited to sending petitions to the British authorities on the other side of the Atlantic Ocean and to organizing in secret a government to put financial pressure on the British, the Second Continental Congress was faced with the problems of conducting a revolution. The tasks faced by the congressional delegates were those of controlling, organizing and supplying a steadily growing American military effort.

Increased Activity in Boston

In Boston, the militia forces that had taken the British garrison under siege were swiftly replaced by the volunteers of what may be called a New England army. Each of the contributing colonies provided a contingent of men under its own commander and undertook to supply its contingent. As far as it went, this plan was adequate, but there was no organized chain of command, and Ward was overall leader only because the other commanders chose to support him. Even so, all important decisions had to be made in council, and this inevitably caused delays. By mid-June, volunteers assisted by militiamen made up the American siege force. But, the enlistment period of the Connecticut volunteers was due to end on December 10, and the other contingents' terms of service would run out at the end of the year. The Americans would probably be unable to force the British to surrender since they could not stop supply ships from entering Boston. Other factors also worked against the Americans: lack of

training, lack of uniforms and other military supplies, shortages of ammunition and bayonets, and the use of many different kinds of muskets which all required different ammunition.

Meanwhile, the British position was steadily improving. On May 25 Gage received reinforcements from England that boosted his strength to 6,500 regulars, and at the same time three generals of very high military reputation arrived. Major Generals Sir John Burgoyne, Sir Henry Clinton, and Sir William Howe were each destined to play

Above: Major General Sir William Howe arrived from Great Britain after the start of the war and commanded the entire British effort.
Opposite, top: Major General Sir Henry Clinton arrived with Howe and also rose to prominence.
Opposite, bottom: Ethan Allen summons Captain de la Place of the 26th Regiment of Foot to surrender Fort Ticonderoga on May 10, 1775.

an important part in the Revolutionary War. The three newly arrived generals quickly came to the conclusion that the British garrison of Boston needed more room to maneuver, for only thus could the superior firepower and discipline of its regulars be used effectively against the Americans. The British generals therefore planned to move forces to Dorchester Heights on the peninsula south of Boston. This position had previously been ignored by both sides, but offered the possibility that artillery on its heights would allow the controlling side to dominate Boston and its approaches.

The Battle of Bunker Hill

News of the British plan reached the Americans, who countered on June 15 by ordering a force of 1,200 men under Colonel William Prescott to move to a position north of the city on the Charlestown peninsula. The American commanders wished to establish a position on Bunker Hill, a rise commanding

Riflemen, armed with accurate, long-range weapons, gave the Americans a small advantage over the British. Robert Magaw describes service in the elite rifle regiment during the Siege of Boston on August 13, 1775

You will Think me Vain should I tell you how much the Riffle men are esteemed their Dress their Arms their Size Strength & activity but Above all their Great eagerness to Attect the Enemy entitle them to the first Rank. the hunting Shirt there is like a full suit at S.t James.s a Riffle man in his Dress may pass Centinels & Go Almost where he pleases while officers of the Other Regiments are Stoped. since we Cam here the Enemy Dare not show their heads. it was Diverting some Days Ago to stand on our Ramparts on prospect Hill and see half a Dozen Riffle men go Down to the Water side & from behind stone walls Chimneys & pop at their floating Batterys at About 300 Yeards Distance tissaid we Killed several. a few shotts from the Riffles always brot on a fire from the flooting Batterys & bunkers Hill where the Enemy are intrenched: but Without any other Effect than to Afford us Amusement

Riflemen led by Daniel Morgan had become skilled killers. Several of the Americans placed themselves in high trees, and, as often as they could distinguish a British officer's uniform, took him off by deliberately aiming at his person. Firing from concealed positions, they took a terrible toll. A British survivor wrote

"Our army," "abounded with young officers, in the subaltern line, and in the course of this unpleasant duty (the burial of the dead) three of the 20th regiment were interred together, the age of the eldest not exceeding seventeen. - In the course of the last action, Lieutenant Hervey, of the 62nd, a youth of sixteen, and nephew of the Adjutant-General of the same name, received several wounds, and was repeatedly ordered off the field by Colonel Anstruther; but his heroic ardor would not allow him to quit the battle, while he could stand and see his brave lads fighting beside him. A ball striking one of his legs, his removal became absolutely necessary, and while they were conveying him away, another wounded him mortally. In this situation the surgeon recommended him to take a powerful dose of opium, to avoid a seven or eight hours' life of most exquisite torture; this he immediately consented to, and when the Colonel entered the tent with Major Harnage, who were both wounded, they asked whether he had any affairs they could settle for him? his reply was, 'that being a minor, everything was already adjusted;' but he had one request, which he had just life enough to utter, "Tell my uncle I died like a soldier."

Left: This somewhat romanticized illustration of a Virginia rifleman in 1775 reveals the main features of this very effective American fighting man.
Below left: A drawing from Harper's Magazine of 1886 shows militiamen bringing gunpowder to the Americans for the Battle of Bunker Hill.
Below right: Americans strengthen their position on Breed's Hill, a 62-ft. height that had been occupied and fortified instead of the 110-ft. Bunker Hill which the American commander, Major General Artemas Ward, had ordered as the main American position on the Charlestown peninsula.

the narrow isthmus connecting the peninsula to the mainland. But on June 16 Prescott's force decided instead to construct a position on Breed's Hill, just outside Charlestown. This position commanded Boston better, but could also be cut off by any British move onto the isthmus behind it. The British were confident that their regulars could not be effectively opposed by the Americans, and after a naval bombardment of the earthworks on the low and vulnerable Breed's Hill at dawn on June 17 an amphibious landing was made by 2,200 men under Howe. The British command felt that the Americans were a "rabble in arms," too poorly led and equipped to warrant anything as formal as a siege. So during the afternoon of June 17 Howe launched a frontal attack against the American redoubt on Breed's Hill, now manned by about 2,200 Americans. The Americans held their fire until the last minute, and then poured down a rain of projectiles that forced the British to pull back. Howe advanced once more against the Americans' front and flanks, and was again pushed back with heavy losses. British reinforcements arrived in time for a third effort, and this time the Americans were short of ammunition and almost wholly lacking in bayonets needed for hand-to-hand fighting. The British thus secured Breed's Hill in this third act of the Battle of Bunker Hill, but to their surprise the Americans managed to pull back in relatively good order. The British losses

The Battle of Bunker Hill was the most important engagement in the first phase of the Revolutionary War. Even though they were supported by the fire of warships, the British were unable to drive the Americans from Breed's Hill. The Americans finally pulled back as they ran out of ammunition.

The Cambridge or the Grand Union Flag was the first official American flag.

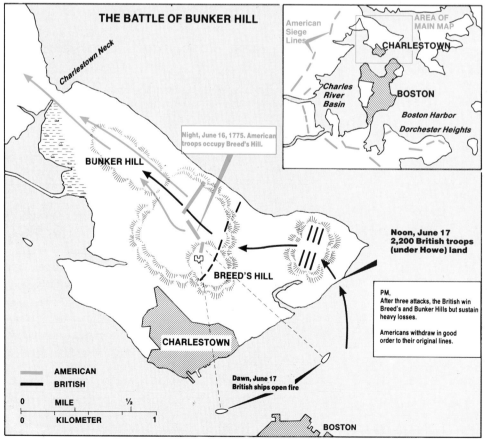

THE BATTLE OF BUNKER HILL

Charlestown Neck

BUNKER HILL

Night, June 16, 1775. American troops occupy Breed's Hill.

BREED'S HILL

CHARLESTOWN

American Siege Lines

AREA OF MAIN MAP

CHARLESTOWN

Charles River Basin

BOSTON

Boston Harbor

Dorchester Heights

Noon, June 17
2,200 British troops
(under Howe) land

PM,
After three attacks, the British win
Breed's and Bunker Hills but sustain
heavy losses.

Americans withdraw in good
order to their original lines.

Dawn, June 17
British ships open fire

BOSTON

AMERICAN
BRITISH

0   MILE   ½
0   KILOMETER   1

The Battle of Bunker Hill, June 17, 1775. A contemporary illustration reveals how the "heights" of Breed's and Bunker Hills command Boston, and therefore why they were so attractive to the British.

War has always produced events that lend themselves to glamorization, and a classic example in the Revolutionary War is the death of Joseph Warren in the Battle of Bunker Hill.

were 1,054, while the American casualties of 440 included 140 dead, 270 wounded and 30 captured.

This was the bloodiest single engagement of the Revolutionary War, and while the result was a tactical victory for the British it was also another boost to American morale. The importance of earthworks in defensive fighting was ignored, and emphasis was placed on the fact that American volunteers had beaten British regulars in two attacks and then been forced back in a third attack only when their ammunition was exhausted. Oddly enough, the long-term results of the Battle of Bunker Hill favored the British rather than the Americans. The British now had a healthy respect for the American soldier, while the Americans built up too optimistic a picture of the abilities of the citizen-soldier against the regular soldier.

Minuteman, Massachusetts Militia (1775)

The Minutemen were the private soldiers of the Alarm Companies formed within provincial militia units to turn out, fully clothed and equipped, "on a minute's notice." The minutemen had no uniform as such, and therefore fought in their civilian clothes, presumably of the type they would wear for hunting. Each man was required to furnish his own musket, together with a bayonet or short sword.

The single most important figure of the American effort in the Revolutionary War is George Washington. Born at Bridges Creek, Virginia, on February 22, 1732, Washington served in the Virginia militia and acquired considerable experience of irregular warfare in the French and Indian War. In June 1775, he was unanimously appointed to command of the Continental Army, a position he held until 1783. In 1789, Washington became the first President of the United States and retired to private life in 1797. He died in his home at Mount Vernon, Virginia, on December 14, 1779.

Revitalized British Effort

After Bunker Hill the British government realized that to retain its American empire a great military effort would be needed. Nearly a year passed before effective plans could be laid and brought into action. Meanwhile the Continental Congress had come to a better understanding of the situation. It realized that it had been forced by matters in New England to assume the leadership of an armed rebellion that could be won only by the con-certed action of the 13 colonies. In overall terms, the Americans still expected a negotiated settlement with Great Britain and hoped that reconciliation was possible, but now saw that armed struggle would also be necessary before any agreement could be reached. The Continental Congress knew that it would take the British several months to lay their plans and send in additional troops. Therefore, they had the time available for the creation of a national army, the consolidation of their slight hold on the government of the 13

Private, Warner's Battalion of the "Green Mountain Boys" (1775)

The "Green Mountain Boys" originated as military companies raised in various New Hampshire and Vermont towns as a result of the disputes between the settlers of the New Hampshire Grants and colonial officials of New York. In June 1775, the Continental Congress combined the companies into a 500-man battalion commanded by Seth Warner. The battalion suffered severely in the Quebec operation and was then re-formed as Warner's Regiment. Like two similar Canadian regiments, the "Green Mountain Boys" were classed separately from the Continental Army's regiments. The illustration shows the standard uniform, to which were often added Indian items such as a wampum pouch and belt, and a tomahawk.

colonies, and the implementation of plans to force the British out of Boston and to invade Quebec. The Americans believed that peace could be re-established by the end of 1776, so they did not plan for a long war.

The Creation of an American Army

The greatest achievement of the Continental Congress was the creation of an American army in the form of the Continental Army. After receiving an appeal from the Massachusetts Provincial Congress, on June 14 the Continental Congress recognized the forces besieging the British in Boston as the Continental Army. At the same time, it decided to raise ten companies of riflemen in Maryland, Pennsylvania, and Virginia as the first soldiers enlisted directly into Continental service. One day later, Colonel George

Washington of Virginia was chosen as commander-in-chief of the Continental Army and commissioned in the rank of major general. The reason for the selection of Washington for the position was not purely military. The Continental Congress knew that the choice of a southerner would help to cement the southern colonies into an alliance for a war then being fought only in a northern colony. On June 16 Washington departed for Boston to assume command of the forces there, which were to be reinforced as soon as possible by six of the new companies of riflemen.

In addition to laying these foundations for the Continental Army, the Continental Congress also began to establish the command structure for a regular army, creating four other major generals and eight brigadier generals to serve under Washington, and establishing staff departments, scales of pay and rations, and articles of war. The choice of the

The Americans based the organization of their army on the European pattern, and thus used the spear as the distinguishing mark and official weapon of junior commissioned officers and senior non-commissioned officers. These weapons are halberds, the variety of spear carrying an axblade on one side, a peak or point (sometimes another axblade) opposite it, and a long spike or blade at the end.

other major generals and the brigadier generals reflected the colonies current situation, so two-thirds of them were New Englanders to acknowledge the fact that the existing army was basically a New England army. Three other officers, Horatio Gates, Charles Lee and Richard Montgomery, were chosen because of their experience in British service. Lee had arrived in America during 1773, and as he was thought to be the ablest officer available he was made Washington's first assistant.

Washington to Supreme Military Command

Washington assumed command of the Continental Army at Cambridge Common on July 3, 1775. At that time, he described his command as a "mixed multitude of people...under very little discipline, order, or government." Washington saw as his most important task the creation of a more formally organized and disciplined army modeled on the British army of the French and Indian War, in which Washington had fought. As Washington put it: "Discipline is the soul of an army. It makes small numbers formidable; procures success for the weak, and esteem to all." Gates, the adjutant general, was responsible for the preparation of orders and regulations, leaving Washington free for the development of discipline, which took the form of regular roll calls and strength returns, and also the discouragement of the tendency of officers and men to come and go as they pleased. Washington did not agree with the "leveling" tendencies of the New Englanders, and because of his belief in the need to distinguish officers from men and to instill a sense of discipline, several types of punishment (pillory, lash, wooden horse and drumming out of camp) were used after the unfortunately large numbers of courts-martial.

These measures were aimed mainly at the existing army. At the same time,

Charles Lee
For further references see pages
47, 48, 55, *56*, 57, 82, *83*, 101, 102

The Continental Army
For further references see pages
26, 27, *32*, 36, 43, 45, 46, 47, *54*, 56, 57, 60, 61, 62, 65, 66, 68, 72, 79, 80, 81, 83, 91, 99, *100*, 101, 102, 104, 110, *113*, 116, 131.

Major General George Washington arrives to take command of the Continental Army at Cambridge Common, Massachusetts, on July 3, 1775.

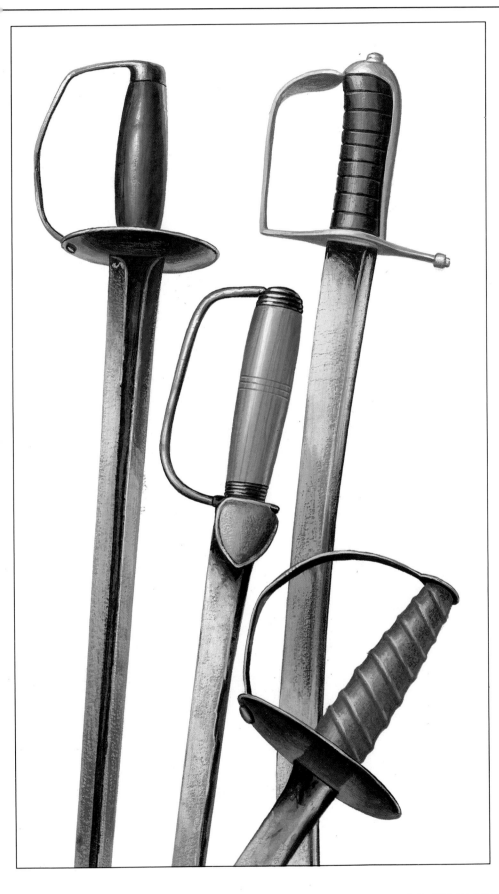

American swords of the Revolutionary War were not as elaborate as those used by the British (see page 41), but were just as effective in a period of change when the sword was losing its importance on the battlefield.

AN APPEAL TO HEAVEN

The ensign of "Washington's Cruisers." This design was at one time a candidate for the official American flag.

Major General Horatio Gates had served with the British army in the French and Indian War. He was chosen as one of Washington's senior subordinates because of the high reputation he had secured in that war.

Washington had to create the new army being enlisted directly into Continental service. In September 1775, a Congressional committee visited Washington's camp. As a result of several meetings the scheme for the new army was set at 26 infantry regiments each containing 728 men, as well as single rifle and artillery regiments. The overall strength of this army was 20,372 men, to be administered, supplied and paid by the Continental Congress up to the end of 1776. With

The most successful American naval captain of the Revolutionary War was John Paul Jones. On December 3, 1775, this outstanding naval officer hoisted on his ship *Alfred* the first U.S. flag flown by an American warship. The flag, the Grand Union (or Cambridge) Flag, contained 13 American stripes with the Union flag in the field. Jones later wrote: ''We cannot be parted in life or death. So long as we can float, we shall float together. If we must sink, we shall go down as one.''

John Paul Jones
For further references see pages 84, 86, 87.

the exception of the hopelessly underestimated term of enlistment, the scheme was workable - at least on paper. In practice, however, Washington found that the officers as much as the men resisted all efforts to create an army that interfered with locally formed units. They were also unwilling to enlist for another year when their first loyalties were with their families and farms. Despite all the pressures that could be brought to bear, on December 10 most of the Connecticut contingent set off for home, and militia from Massachusetts and New Hampshire had to be brought in to plug the gap in the line besieging the British in Boston. Three weeks later the enlistments of several other contingents expired, and many more men left.

The Importance of Militia Units

So on January 1, 1776, when the army formally became "Continental in every respect," Washington found that instead of 20,000 men under command he had only 8,000, a number that increased to only 9,000 by early March. This meant that

the shortfall had to be made up with militia units. By now it had become clear that the initial enlistment of the Continental Army for one year only meant that the whole distressing, disrupting process would have to be repeated at the end of the year.

At this time, Washington was pressing ahead with the siege of Boston. his administrative and personal leadership skills began to show strongly as the army slowly overcame all types of supply failings. The commander-in-chief put small parties of men on board American ships which then succeeded in capturing a useful number of British supply vessels.

October 13, 1775, can be regarded as the birthday of the modern U.S. Navy. On that day, the Continental Congress authorized the fitting out of two ships to intercept vessels carrying stores to the British forces in North America. Precursors of this Continental Navy were "Washington's Cruisers." The first was commissioned on September 5, 1775, as the initial regularly commissioned warship in American service, the schooner *Hannah*. She sailed on the day she was commissioned and, two days later, took the *Unity*, the first naval prize taken in the Revolutionary War. The *Hannah* was soon joined by one brigantine and five more schooners. All flew a variation on the "Liberty Tree" ensign, one of the candidates as the first official American flag. On December 13, 1775, the Continental Congress authorized the construction of 13 frigates (five of 32 guns each, five of 28 guns each and three of 24 guns each) for the Continental Navy. Only seven were completed, and all of them were lost in the Revolutionary War. The first commander of the Continental Navy was Esek Hopkins (left), who was appointed on December 22, 1775 but cashiered less than two years later for failure to follow the orders of the Continental Navy.

By the beginning of the fourth quarter of the 18th century the spear was out of date as a first-line military weapon, but still retained a small niche in the British army. In this force the spear (in a number of forms with a variety of names such as pike, half-pike and spontoon) was used as an emblem of the rank and function. The visibility of the tall weapon was supposed to allow soldiers, even in the haze and tumult of battle, to find both the commissioned and senior non-commissioned officers who carried them. In fact the spears were seldom carried in the Revolutionary War.

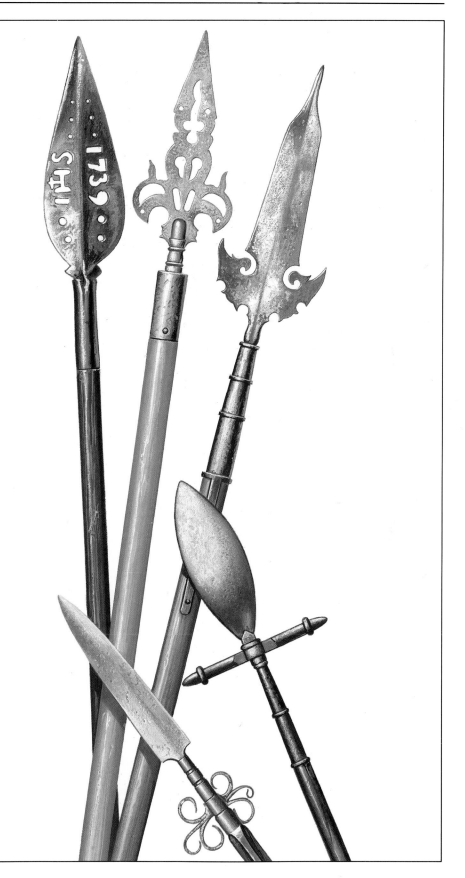

An American merchant flag, used until the 1790s; the colors could vary.

The most successful of these raiding groups was that of Commodore Esek Hopkins. He led six converted merchantmen from Philadelphia, on February 17. They sailed to the Bahamas, where New Providence was attacked and men put ashore to capture cannon and ammunition before the ships returned to Providence, Rhode Island. On March 19 the Continental Congress authorized privateering, and this became a major feature of the Revolutionary War as American ships attacked British shipping on the vital Atlantic routes and elsewhere. At about the same time the Continental Congress and several colonies sponsored purchasing missions to the Dutch and French possessions in the West Indies, where significant amounts of war materiel were bought. In 1776, Spain also began to sell munitions to the Americans.

Washington also dispatched Colonel Henry Knox, later his Chief of Artillery, to the captured Fort Ticonderoga, and during the winter of 1775-76 Knox returned to Cambridge, Massachusetts over icebound or even nonexistent roads with about 50 pieces of artillery. By March 1776 Washington was well enough equipped to push forward against the British defenders of Boston.

The Invasion of Quebec

In many respects, the siege of Boston was only a sideshow to the main American effort of the period. This took the form of an invasion of Quebec, which the Americans saw as a fourteenth British colony that might rebel. It was an apparently vulnerable target whose loss would deprive the British of its major overland invasion route along the line of rivers and lakes between Montreal and New York. The Continental Congress got nowhere with its appeal for the inhabitants of Quebec to join the American cause, and in June 1775, ordered Major General Philip Schuyler of New York to seize Quebec if it was ''practicable'' and ''not disagreeable'' to the inhabitants.

Schuyler managed to create a 2,000-man core for what later became known as the Northern Army. In September 1775, he

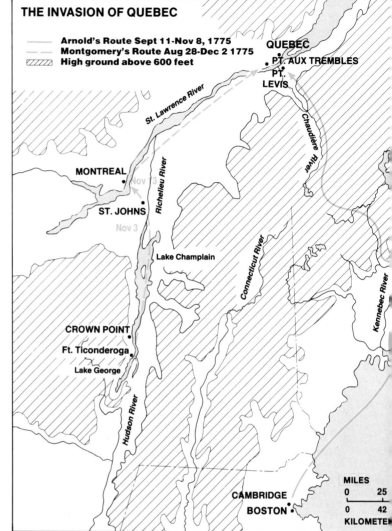

THE INVASION OF QUEBEC

—— Arnold's Route Sept 11-Nov 8, 1775
— — Montgomery's Route Aug 28-Dec 2 1775
▨▨▨ High ground above 600 feet

departed at the head of this force from Fort Ticonderoga with the object of taking Montreal before advancing down the St. Lawrence toward the city of Quebec. To provide a second prong to this invasion, Washington dispatched Benedict Arnold and a force of 1,100 men, including a rifle contingent under Captain Daniel Morgan of Virginia, for an extremely imaginative parallel stroke. Arnold left Cambridge on September 12 for an advance that was to take his force up the Kennebec River and across the wilds of Maine before moving down the Chaudiere River to link up with Schuyler's force outside Quebec.

Schuyler made good progress at first, but was then delayed by the stubborn 600-man British defense of Fort St. Johns where the Americans had to leave the

The American attack on Quebec in the closing months of 1775 was poorly conceived and badly executed. It was notable, however, for the classic march through the Maine wilderness by Benedict Arnold's detachment.

Richelieu River and strike northwest to Montreal. Fort St. Johns was taken under siege on September 6, and when Schuyler became ill on September 13, his place was taken by Brigadier General Richard Montgomery. Fort St. Johns finally surrendered on November 2, and Montgomery's force advanced to Montreal. Ethan Allen had already made a disastrous effort to take Montreal and been captured in the process, but on November 13 Montgomery took the city and captured a British river flotilla. The British governor general, Sir Guy Carleton, pulled back to Quebec.

Brigadier General Richard Montgomery headed the main American force involved in the abortive invasion of Canada in the fall and early winter of 1775.

A Classic March through the Maine Wilderness

Five days earlier, Arnold had reached Levis at the mouth of the Chaudiere River opposite Quebec. Arnold's approach march remains one of military history's classics of endurance and determination under adverse geographical and climatic conditions. One part of his force turned back, and Arnold's force was further reduced by starvation, disease, drowning, and desertion. On November 13 Arnold's remaining 600 men crossed the St. Lawrence and, copying General James Wolfe's 1759 maneuver that led to the British capture of Quebec from the French, scaled the cliffs and camped on the Heights of Abraham. As the French had done in 1759, the British regulars and Quebec militia retired into the city. The American force was too small even to consider an assault when the British refused to fight on open ground.

Arnold finally pulled back up the St. Lawrence to Point aux Trembles, where he was joined on December 3 by Montgomery and 300 men, all that could be spared from the American garrison at Montreal. Montgomery then assumed overall command. The American commander was faced by total indifference on the part of the French and by steady loyalty to the crown on the part of the British. He also had to take into consideration the fact that the enlistment of about half his force was due to expire. In an attempt to win a decisive victory while he could, Montgomery launched a desperate attack on Quebec during the night of December 30. The attack was made in a raging snowstorm and was defeated by the numerically superior British, who could call on 1,800 men. In the fight Montgomery was killed and Arnold wounded, and American losses totaled 100 killed and wounded in addition to 300 captured.

The Americans Are Driven Back

Despite his wound and lack of numbers, Arnold tried to keep up the illusion of a

This heroic painting of Montgomery's death in the disastrous American attack on Quebec during December 30, 1775, provides little indication of the real conditions: of bitter cold and driving snow as the outnumbered Americans sought vainly to oust a well prepared and ably led British garrison.

siege to buy time for the arrival of reinforcements, which appeared in the form of Continental Army regiments from New Jersey, New York and Pennsylvania. But they arrived by the handful rather than as a single force. Decimated by smallpox and several other diseases, and never adequately supplied with ammunition, clothing and food over their dreadful lines of communication, the 8,000 Americans eventually committed to the Quebec campaign were never in any real position to take the offensive. The British too were reinforced, but on an altogether more sensible basis. Burgoyne arrived on May 6 with forces that were large by local standards. In June 1776 Burgoyne went on the offensive against an American force that was now under the command of Major General John Sullivan, but already beginning to disintegrate. Sullivan attempted to stabilize the American position with an

attack on Trois Rivieres during June 6, but the 2,000 Americans under Brigadier General John Thomas had been deceived by faulty intelligence and instead of a 600-man garrison found Burgoyne with 8,000 men. The Americans were utterly dispersed, and Sullivan, realizing that his position was no longer tenable, abandoned Montreal and fell back first to Crown Point and by mid-July to Ticonderoga. In the north, the strategic initiative had passed firmly to the British.

Lake Champlain, the Key

Both sides knew that control of Lake Champlain would decide the outcome of the obvious next move for the British, an advance into New York. Each side therefore rushed to create a small flotilla of warships, with the American effort

Major General John Sullivan was one of the senior American commanders in the New York campaign.

coordinated by Arnold. The British flotilla was manned by sailors from the transport ships that had brought Burgoyne's force up the St. Lawrence River, and its ships were more heavily armed than their American counterparts. On October 28, the Battle of Valcour Island occurred. The British ships attacked the American flotilla and sank or destroyed most of them. Arnold managed to slip away with the survivors, but was caught at Split Rock where the rest of the American flotilla was destroyed. Yet Arnold's effort had saved the day for the Americans: the campaign for control of Lake Champlain had so delayed the British that winter overtook them. The British did briefly occupy Crown Point at the southern end of Lake

Champlain, but then pulled back into Quebec for the winter.

Farther east, the Americans had enjoyed better fortunes in the first half of 1776. By spring 1776 Washington felt that his forces were in a position to move against the British garrison of Boston. The American commander-in-chief launched his effort on March 4 with a move onto the Dorchester Heights. The reinforced American artillery was emplaced to threaten the city, and a few days later Washington ordered the fortification of Nook's Hill, a point even closer to Boston. The British had already realized the impossibility of holding Boston for much longer. Howe, Gage's successor as British commander, had also concluded

Major General Sir William Howe
For further references see pages
16, 19, 39, 42, 47, 49, 50, 51, *52*, 53, 55, 56, 57, 60, 61, 62, 64, 65, 66, *67*, 70, 79, 81, 83, 113.

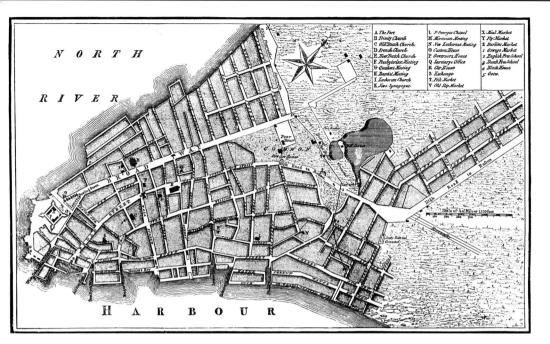

A The Fort
B Trinity Church
C Old Dutch Church
D French Church
E New Dutch Church
F Presbyterian Meeting
G Quakers Meeting
H Baptist Meeting
I Lutheran Church
K Jews Synagogue

L St Georges Chapel
M Moravian Meeting
N New Lutheran Meeting
O Custom House
P Governors House
Q Secretarys Office
R City House
S Exchange
T Fish Market
V Old Slip Market

X Meal Market
Y Fly Market
Z Burling Market
1 Oswego Market
2 English Free School
3 Dutch Free School
4 Block House
5 Gate.

Above: A map of New York during the Revolutionary War provides striking evidence of how small all American cities were at the time. The city was vitally important, but occupied only the southernmost tip of Manhattan Island.
Right: The American siege of Boston was not pressed with great severity even under Washington's personal command, but Howe still decided that the city was a poor base for American operations and completed the evacuation of his force by March 17, 1776.

that Boston was a poor strategic base from which to retain the American colonies. Howe had been holding Boston only until the arrival of the transports needed for the British evacuation to Halifax in Nova Scotia, but finally pulled out under the increasing American pressure. In Halifax, Howe intended to await reinforcement as he planned the capture of a new British base of operations in the 13 colonies.

American Advantages From the British Loss of Boston

Despite the fact that the British had planned their evacuation of Boston, the Americans did benefit materially from their seizure of the city, for Washington's forces gladly accepted the artillery and ammunition that the British had been unable to remove. More important,

Captain George Pausch was a German soldier hired by the British to fight in North America. He and his men left their homes in 1776. Many never returned.

Pausch's Journal: 1776 May 15,

In conformity to the order of our Gracious Prince the roll-call was beaten at half-past three P. M., and the company marched out of the Mill-fortification to the Parade-ground, where all the necessary accoutrements for my men were found in readiness. A quarter of an hour afterwards, the signal was given by the tap of the drum for a forward movement; and, the lines being formed, we at once marched through the hospital Gate of the old town to the wood-warehouses. Here the company immediately embarked on the ships, which had been designated for our transportation, in the presence of our most gracious sovereigns.

Pausch and his men crossed the Atlantic aboard a leaky, unseaworthy ship that formerly had been a slave trading ship. It was a miserable journey.

Toward 4 o'clock in the morning of the 15th this gale was succeeded by a favorable wind which lasted till the 17th, when by 4 o'clock in the morning it threatened to change into a most furious gale. Indeed, it soon became so violent, that the Captain, who was generally a most courageous man and a daring mariner, lost his courage. So, also, did the sailors. All the sails which were hoisted were torn by the wind into tatters, and the main mast (the strongest) was broken short off. Each successive wave following the other swept over the deck or rather the ship; and so much water came into the vessel, that those who slept in the lowest bunk under the forward deck with their baggage, were flooded; and this, too although all the openings and air-holes (dead lights) were covered. Now the ship would lay on one side, and now on the other - her masts touching the waters, which now rose around the ship higher than the masts. At times we seemed to be in a deep abyss between the walls of water. Every one of us, including the Captain himself, expected every moment would be our last; and each one

appeared reconciled to the inevitable, giving up all hope of ever seeing America, or his fatherland again.

Pausch and his artillerymen eventually arrived in Canada where they joined Burgoyne's invasion of New York. Pausch's cannon, along with the Hessian infantry, saved the hard pressed British forces at the Battle of Freeman's Farm, 19 September, 1777.

The firing seemed to draw nearer; from which one might infer that our right wing was retreating. Accordingly, we left our position, and marched for about a quarter of an hour in the direction of the firing. We then formed in line of battle, I placing the two cannon in the road which led into the woods. The fences, which lay to my left, I had already quickly thrown down in order that the enemy, on his approach, might not hide behind them.

Meanwhile, Major von Geismar, who was yet on the staff of Gen. Riedesel, was sent by the latter to see if there was any possibility of reaching Gen. Burgoyne and informing him that he stood here in readiness with his own Regiment, two companies of the Regiment Rhetz and two 6 pound cannon, and that he was only waiting for orders to reinforce him. In the meantime, the patrols returned one after the other. The second patrol having reported that the communication between us and the troops in action was open, the General (Riedesel) marched at once toward the right.

He choose this way, in order to make a division on the right flank of the enemy. He also ordered the march to be beaten on the drums, which caused the men to cheer repeatedly. After descending the hill we met von Geismar on his return with orders from Gen. Burgoyne directing Gen. Riedesel to attack the enemy on their right flank, and, if possible, to follow them up. This, however, we were prevented from doing both by the woods and the swamps behind which the enemy were hidden. I was also to go to the right wing of the 21st English regiment.

Under a shower of the enemy's bullets, I safely reached the hill just as the 21st and 9th Regiments were about to abandon it.

Nevertheless, I continued to drag my two cannon up the hill, while Gen. Phillips exhorted the English Regiments, and the officers their men, to face the enemy. English captains and other officers and privates and also the Brunswick Chasseurs, which happened to be detailed here, grasped the ropes. The entire line of these regiments faced about, and by this faithful assistance, my cannon were soon on top of the hill. I had shells Rev 3-4 brought up and placed by the side of the cannon; and as soon as I go the range, I fired twelve or fourteen shots in quick succession into the foe who were within good pistol shot distance.

The firing from muskets was at once renewed, and assumed lively proportions particularly the platoon fire from the left wing of Riedesel. Presently, the enemy's fire, though very lively at one time, suddenly ceased. I advanced about sixty paces sending a few shells after the flying enemy, and firing from twelve to fifteen shots more into the woods into which they had retreated. Everything then became quiet; and about fifteen minutes afterwards darkness set in.

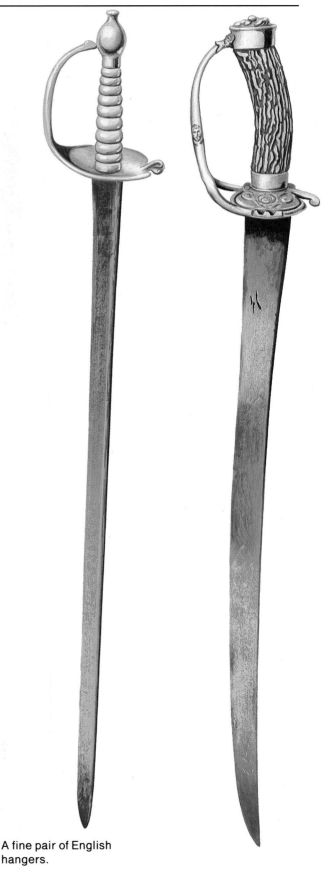

A fine pair of English hangers.

however, was the boost to American morale at a time when it was being battered by the news from the Quebec front. Washington expected that the British would now move against New York and started to move his forces into this area. This was what Howe was planning, and the British forces in Halifax were reinforced for the effort, which was to be supported by a fleet commanded by Howe's brother, Admiral Sir Richard Howe.

For the immensely difficult task of subduing the American colonies 3,000 miles across the Atlantic Ocean, Sir William Howe requested reinforcement to a strength of 50,000 men. Such a figure was impossibly large for the British government to find, yet during 1776 Howe's strength rose to more than 30,000 men. These troops included an increasingly large number of German mercenaries recruited largely from Hesse-Kassel, which during the course of the Revolutionary War provided about 30,000 men including officers up to the rank of major general.

Though there was in general a uniformity of pattern in the swords of each regiment, officers often carried their own swords. These German weapons show great variation in overall design as well as in detail of decoration, and some of the more ingenious had features such as a saw-back.

Richtige Abbildung der von den amerikanischen Provinzialisten belagerten und wiedereroberten Hauptstadt und Festung Boston in Amerika, im Monat Merz 1776.

A German illustration of the British seaborne retreat from Boston considerably overemphasizes the heights overlooking the city.

The Declaration of Independence

It was now clear that the British were not prepared to accommodate American desires for greater liberty and rights within the British empire. A great British effort was clearly underway to reduce the American colonies to their original status, and the only other possibility open to the Americans was complete independence from Great Britain. The Declaration of Independence on July 4, 1776, thus established the new nation. At the same time, it turned the limited rebellion to secure rights for the Americans under the British flag into a war for independence. All sensible men now saw that a major and sustained national effort would be required. The tasks facing the new nation were enormous. With a population of perhaps 2.5 million, the 13 new states had a pool of manpower greater than the British could hope to maintain in any practical manner on the western side of the Atlantic. However, about 20 percent of this population were black and in general slaves not eligible for service, about 35 percent of the rest remained loyal to the British, and there was also a sizeable

percentage of fence-sitters. Of those able to serve in the army, most were farmers with large families to support and land to tend, a fact that made long-term recruitment all but impossible. Other factors against American independence were lack of any real industrial base and poor communications. Lack of an industrial base meant that the Continental Army had to rely on captured British equipment or supplies from friendly European powers brought in through a tightening British blockade. American communications generally ran up and down rivers, and along the coast: the former made transportation very difficult between what had now become different states, especially when the British blockade effectively prevented coastal movement.

Another factor that made it difficult for the Americans to fight a successful war against the British was the nature of the government that came into being in 1776. The very limited central government had only the smallest power, whereas each state government jealously retained its already extensive powers. The Continental Congress continued as a meeting place for states' delegates, but lacked any powers

The single most decisive episode in American history was the signing of the Declaration of Independence on July 4, 1776. This declared that the United States of America was "free and independent ... absolved from any allegiance to the British Crown."

of its own or an executive to carry out its enactments. Shortly after the Declaration of Independence, in an effort to provide the Continental Congress with limited but specific powers, Articles of Confederation were drawn up. However it was only in 1781 that the Articles were ratified by the states, which remained extremely jealous of their rights despite the near disasters that had overtaken the fledgling United States because of its lack of a workable central government. The Continental Congress meanwhile exercised many of the powers granted by the Articles, but lacked the power to tax or to raise military forces. All the Continental Congress could do,

therefore, was set quotas for the states to meet on the basis of their wealth and population. The Continental Congress lacked the power to compel the individual states to meet their quota requirements, which were almost never met.

Washington's Problem

In these circumstances, it is not surprising that Washington never got the army he needed, in either size or composition. Numbers of men and equipment were always below the requirement, and state militia units often had to be used to

bolster the strength of the Continental Army. This put Washington in a vicious circle of declining numbers: when the Continental Army needed militia reinforcement at dire moments, the militiamen were less willing to serve and the position of the Continental Army was worsened, making it even less likely that militia reinforcement would be forthcoming. Even when militia forces were made available to the Continental Army, the system was highly inefficient in terms of appointments, supplies, and lines of communication.

Washington remained opposed to the concept of reinforcing the Continental Army with state militia and by early 1776 had decided that success could be provided only by an enlarged Continental Army enlisted for the duration of the war. The commander-in-chief finally persuaded the Continental Congress that his idea was right, and in October 1776, it voted for a new Continental Army establishment of 88 infantry battalions totaling about 60,000 men, enlisted for three years or "during the present war" with each state to provide men in accordance with the quota established in the Articles. After the November 1776 retreat across New Jersey the Continental Congress voted an additional 22 battalions to be recruited

An illustration of 1876 provides portraits and autograph signatures of the men who formulated and signed the Declaration of Independence in Philadelphia on July 4, 1776.

directly by the Continental Army. This 110-battalion establishment remained in force until 1781, when it was trimmed to a 59-battalion establishment.

But this was all on paper. In practice Washington never had more than 30,000 men under command. In only a few battles was Washington ever able to field as many as 15,000 men. This was a very serious limitation on the commander-in-chief's ability to wage the war for independence. It must be admitted, however, that the Americans would have been very hard pressed to equip a Continental Army at full establishment strength, and that the small size of the Continental Army placed less strain on an already overburdened supply system.

Washington's Greatest Achievement

Almost certainly Washington's greatest Achievements were the creation of any type of Continental Army at all and then its

maintenance in the field. The result was a peculiarly American army that never developed into the image of the British army as Washington originally desired, but which ultimately proved effective for the type of war in which it evolved.

The Continental Army lived and fought in three territorial divisions or departments under the overall leadership of Washington. The main army was that under Washington himself in the middle states, while the Northern Army operated in northern New York and the Southern Army in the Carolinas and Georgia. Washington was in many respects a commander in name only as far as the Northern and Southern Armies were concerned, for the Continental Congress appointed their commanders and issued orders directly to them. Up to 1777 the Northern Army was more important by far than the Southern Army, which existed only on paper. By 1780 the situation was completely reversed as the British shifted their main effort to the south.

The Continental Army consisted mainly

Charleston

For further references
see pages
49, 50, 90, 91, *93*, 94,
95, *96*, 102, 104, 111,
112, 114, 125, 126,
130.

Major General Sir Henry Clinton

For further references
see pages
16, *49*, 57, 73, 81, 82,
87, 89, 90, 94, 95, 101,
102, *103*, 104, 111,
113, 114, 116, 117,
118, 121, 125, 128.

of infantry and artillery, and possessed virtually no cavalry. The basic infantry unit was the regiment or battalion of eight companies. Such units were grouped in differing numbers into a brigade commanded by a brigadier general. Several brigades formed a division commanded by a major general. The four regiments of artillery constituted the artillery brigade commanded by Brigadier General Henry Knox, but for tactical purposes the artillery companies were distributed among the infantry units.

At the same time that the Continental Army was beginning to take shape, the Continental Congress was trying to provide an American navy. The building of 13 frigates was authorized in 1776, but the strength of the British navy was overwhelming and completely dominated maritime matters until the advent of French sea power later in the war.

Lack of British Strategy

The British failed to develop a consistent strategy throughout the war, which meant that they operated on a year-to-year basis. Washington could not develop a comprehensive strategy either, but, he did develop an operational plan, a consistent line of action, that successfully exploited British weakness. He kept his main force in a central position to block any British advance into the American interior, he considered very carefully whether or not to offer battle for limited objectives, he always made sure that his army could not be destroyed in its entirety, and he always tried to find a method of concentrating his forces for the decisive moment when the British were spread too thin. Ironically, Washington understood more fully than the British the importance of naval power. In the long term this allowed Washington to exploit a naval victory by his French allies to strike the decisive blow.

The nearest that the British came to a consistent strategic objective throughout the war was the securing of the Lake Champlain/Hudson River line as a means of dividing the colonies. The British expected that this would allow them to reach agreement with the less inflamed Americans in the middle and southern colonies and then concentrate their military effort against the New Englanders who had started the war. For the 1776 campaign, therefore, Howe decided to use Great Britain's undisputed mastery of the sea to move the British strength from Halifax to New York, where a base would be secured before the British advanced up the Hudson River/Lake Champlain line. With commendable military sense, Howe felt that the full British strength should be used for the New York operation. In a manner typical of the divided British control of the war, however, the authorities in London had already sent a substantial number of men for operations in Quebec. Howe decided on another division of strength, for according to ex-governors of southern colonies taking refuge in British ships off the coast of the southern states, loyalists in this region needed only limited support before they would rise and reinstate British rule.

War in the South

This last adventure was entrusted to Admiral Sir Peter Parker. His squadron was so delayed in its arrival from England toward the end of May that loyalist uprisings in the Carolinas and Virginia had already been defeated. In December 1775, Virginia rebels had defeated loyalists in a minor engagement at Great Bridge near Norfolk, and the British governor had fled to the safety of a British warship lying offshore, from which he sent reports to London of the willingness of the loyalists to oust the rebels. More significantly, on February 27, 1776 a force of 1,100 North Carolinians had defeated about 1,800 loyalists in the Battle of Moores Creek Bridge as the loyalists were marching on Wilmington in the hope of establishing a British coastal base.

Despite such failures, Parker decided to attack Charleston, the largest city in the south, using Clinton's force which had been earmarked for the proposed base at Wilmington. The vulnerability of Charleston was fully appreciated by Washington, who sent Lee south to organize the defenses of the city with the South

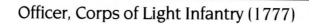

Officer, Corps of Light Infantry (1777)

In the summer of 1777, Washington created a regimental-size Corps of Light Infantry using men detached from existing regiments. This illustration shows an officer of the corps (distinguishable by his spontoon, crimson sash, and silver rather than white worsted epaulets) with the red facings that distinguished men of the southern group of mid-Atlantic states (Delaware, Maryland, Pennsylvania, and Virginia).

Colonel William Moultrie was the commander of the seaward defense of Charleston, South Carolina, on June 28, 1776. On this date, the American fort on Sullivan's Island, constructed of palmetto logs and sand, soaked up the British cannon fire without suffering major damage, and then used its artillery to severely damage the ships of Admiral Sir Peter Parker's squadron. The result was the withdrawal of Major General Sir Henry Clinton's force, which had been entrusted with the capture of Charleston.

Carolina militia and newly raised Continental forces. Against Lee's advice, the South Carolinians based their defense on Fort Moultrie, a palmetto fort built on Sullivan's Island commanding the approach to Charleston harbor. In purely tactical sense, this was the wrong place to locate the main defense of the city, but the American error was remedied by the faulty British assault, which was planned and executed too hastily. Clinton's troops landed on neighboring Long Island, but could not take any active part in the Battle of Sullivan's Island on June 28 because the water was too deep for them to wade across to Sullivan's Island. So when Parker's ships tried to pass Sullivan's Island and enter Charleston harbor they were devastated by the American artillery under Colonel William Moultrie. Parker sensibly extracted his squadron, and shortly afterward, Clinton's men were lifted off Long Island for transport to New York, where they came under Howe's command.

For the next three years, the British ignored the southern states. Yet there were undoubtedly many southern loyalists who would have supported a British effort in the region.

The British Invade New York

There has long been a tendency to depict the more famous historical figures of the Revolutionary War as ordinary men responding to challenge. Israel Putnam had acquired a considerable reputation as a middle-ranking officer in the British colonial forces involved in the French and Indian War, but this idealized picture shows him leaving his plow to become one of Washington's most important subordinates with the rank of major general.

Between March and June Howe had waited at Halifax for his reinforcements, which were severely delayed by the weather. Toward the end of June, Howe decided that he could wait no longer and embarked in his brother's fleet for New York. On July 2, Howe's army landed on Staten Island, where it waited for reinforcement. Ordered by the Continental Congress to hold New York, Washington had only 19,000 men and was faced with the problems of countering a land attack, a naval attack, or both. Here Washington made the same mistake as the South Carolinians at Charleston: he concentrated his defense as far forward as possible. Major earthworks were thrown up on the Brooklyn Heights, and batteries of artillery were established on Governor's Island and Staten Island. While half of Washington's army held Manhattan Island, the other half under Major General Nathanael Greene took up positions across the Flatbush area of Long Island. Greene succumbed to malaria and was replaced by Major General John Sullivan, but at the last moment Washington installed Major General Israel Putnam over Sullivan. Washington's command was too far forward and also divided. The only land communication to Manhattan Island from the mainland was over the Kingsbridge at the northern tip of the island, farthest from the settlement of New York at the southern end. Here, though, the British did not make the tactical mistake that defeated them at Sullivan's Island.

By mid-August, Howe had been reinforced to a strength of 32,000 men, including 9,000 Hessians, but knew that the campaigning season was too advanced for his full Hudson River/Lake Champlain operation. The British commander decided to take New York to provide his force with adequate winter quarters as well as a base for the Hudson River/Lake Champlain operation to be undertaken in the following year.

Above: British movement up the Hudson River by boat was barred by a chainlink barrier across the river near West Point.
Above right: Another of Washington's most important subordinates in the New York campaign was Major General Nathanael Greene.

On August 22, the British started to land on Long Island after crossing The Narrows and by August 25 had pushed 20,000 men onto Long Island. Knowing that Putnam was positioned to defend the approaches to the shore of Long Island offering the shortest crossing to New York, Howe pinned the American left and right wings (commanded respectively by Sullivan and Brigadier General William Alexander). His main strength passed across the American front to outflank and attack the Americans' left wing in the Battle of Long Island on August 27. The American forward positions crumpled, and they fled back to their main position on the Brooklyn Heights: American losses were 200 killed and 1,000 taken

prisoner while the British suffered 400 casualties. Half of Washington's army would probably have been destroyed if Howe had pursued vigorously, but in the military fashion of the period, he halted at nightfall, camped and prepared for a methodical assault over the next few days. Washington did not wait for the British assault to develop, and during the night of August 29-30, he evacuated the Long Island force, which crossed the East River to New York in boats manned by the fishermen of Colonel John Glover's Marblehead Regiment. It was a brilliantly planned and executed evacuation, but could have ended in disaster if the British naval forces had intervened. According to some sources, the wind was against them,

Above: Brigadier General William Stirling's American left-flank force withdraws across Cowann's Creek toward Brooklyn in the closing stages of the Battle of Long Island on August 27, 1776. The retreat was typical of American reverses at a time when Major General Sir William Howe was showing an astute tactical skill in his leadership of the British.

Left: Artillery was vitally important to each side in the Revolutionary War. After the Battle of Long Island, the American guns were carefully evacuated as Washington's army moved south to New York.

The evacuation of the American forces from Long Island to New York on August 29-30, 1776, was planned with great skill and carried out brilliantly. Washington, seen here directing operations from his horse, was the last American to leave the Brooklyn shore.

but others reported that the Americans put obstacles in the river.

The Battle of White Plains

Washington now had two weeks to complete his defenses of Manhattan Island as Howe prepared his next move, a landing in Kip's Bay on September 15. The Connecticut militia holding this area broke and ran, and if Howe had quickly pressed ahead he could have reached the western shore of Manhattan Island without difficulty and so divided the American force in two. But on reaching the middle of the island Howe paused until the rest of his force had landed. This gave Putnam just enough time to pull his men out of New York and slip up the west side of the island into the main defensive position. Here the Battle of Harlem Heights was fought on September 16, and Washington checked Howe's advance.

Washington knew that the Harlem Heights position was dangerously exposed to a British outflanking movement by water. This became clear on October 18

when four British brigades began to land at Pell's Point on the western shore of Long Island Sound, northeast of Washington's position and well in its rear. Washington pulled his men back to White Plains, but left 6,000 men in Fort Washington on the northern end of Manhattan Island and in Fort Lee just across the Hudson River.

On October 28 Howe launched a probing attack on Washington's latest position, but was initially repulsed in this so-called Battle of White Plains. As the day wore on, the determination of the American resistance began to flag, and the British regular troops finally drove the Americans from the field. Washington had already foreseen the futility of continued resistance against the militarily superior British, and thus the Americans were already pulling back up the eastern bank of the Hudson River toward the New York highlands. Washington expected that the British would press hard on his heels, but Howe again outmaneuvered the American commander-in-chief. The British commander felt that there was little value in pursuing the remnant of the American army more than 20 miles north of New York, and instead turned southwest to Dobb's Ferry on the eastern bank of the Hudson River and thereby isolated Fort Washington from any chance of overland retreat to the north.

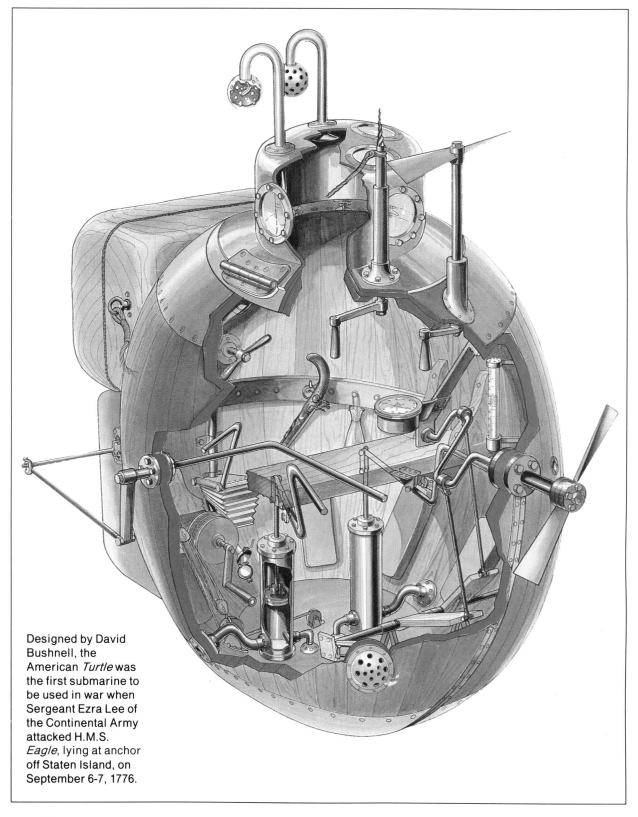

Designed by David Bushnell, the American *Turtle* was the first submarine to be used in war when Sergeant Ezra Lee of the Continental Army attacked H.M.S. *Eagle*, lying at anchor off Staten Island, on September 6-7, 1776.

The New York campaign of 1776 was a major failure for American arms, and led to Washington's retreat through New Jersey to the Delaware River and the temporary safety of Pennsylvania.

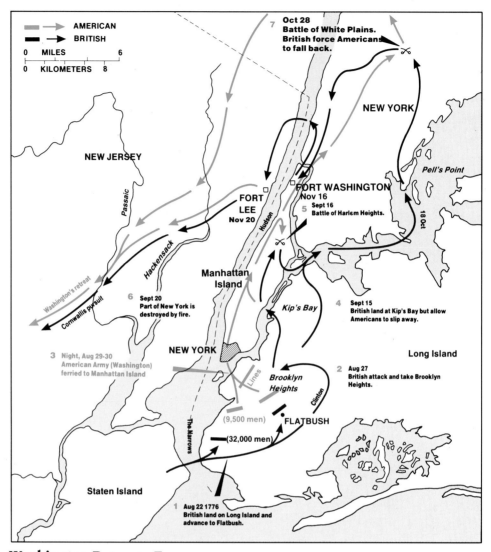

Washington Retreats From New York

Greene had now recovered from his bout of malaria and advised Washington to maintain a defense in the two Hudson River forts. Washington agreed and also decided to split his command. Major Generals Lee and William Heath were left on the New York side of the Hudson River with about 8,000 men to prevent any British advance into the New York highlands by holding the passes at North Castle and Peekskill. Washington himself led the remaining 5,000 American fighting men across the Hudson River into New Jersey.

Howe was biding his time, and on November 16, he made his effort against Fort Washington. With the aid of a bombardment from British warships on the river, the British infantry successfully stormed the fort, capturing 3,000 Americans and large quantities of materiel. Greene decided that it was no longer worth defending Fort Lee, which was evacuated on November 18. The Americans could not take the artillery, ammunition and stores held in the fort with them, and everything that could not be destroyed fell into the hands of the grateful British.

Washington Crosses the Delaware

Pressure on the Americans falling back

Above: Major General Charles Lee had been ordered to pull back across the Delaware River to join Washington, but delayed in the hope of catching the British unawares in New Jersey. He was trapped at Morristown on December 12, 1776, and surrendered to Lieutenant Colonel Harcourt.

through New Jersey was maintained by a detachment under Major General Lord Cornwallis, who had been detached by Howe with the specific purpose of harrying Washington. By the end of November, the American forces were in full retreat south across New Jersey toward the Delaware River. Cornwallis's detachment pressed them from river barrier to river barrier - first the Hackensack, then the Passaic and Raritan, and finally the Millstone. Lee and his 4,000 men had been ordered to join Washington south of the Delaware River in Pennsylvania, and thus constituted a rearguard for Washington's force. An experienced ex-British colonel, Lee was becoming increasingly concerned with Washington's handling of strategic matters, writing to Gates that "...a certain great man is most damnably deficient..." Lee deliberately delayed his retreat in the belief that his force could operate within New Jersey, worrying the British so seriously with raids that the American position would be restored. But Lee was quickly trapped at Morristown, and after a short delay, he surrendered on December 12 with about half of his men. The one

as he tried to decide what to do next. On the day that Lee surrendered near Morristown, the Continental Congress decided that Pennsylvania would probably be the next target of the British, and hurriedly left Philadelphia for Baltimore, Maryland. The Continental Congress also decided that the desperate state of American affairs called for desperate measures, and on the same day, Washington was voted almost dictatorial powers in an effort to keep the revolution alive.

It was not just the British who were causing trouble for Washington. During this period, his army was also melting away around him. Whole companies of attached militia forces left together, and the Continental Army was hard hit by desertions. The same applied to the 8,000-man force left to guard against a British push into the New York highlands, where the American commanders were becoming increasingly concerned that the enlistment of their men would expire at the end of the year, giving them every legal right to return home regardless of the desperate military situation.

The British were fully aware of

Right: A stern Washington supervises the Continental Army's crossing of the Delaware River.

useful result of Lee's ambition was the additional breathing space it gave to Washington in his retreat to the Delaware River. He halted in early December to regroup and rest his surviving 2,000 men

Washington's problems and confidently expected that the arrival of the new year would see the total disintegration of the American forces and the collapse of the ''American rebellion.'' Howe therefore ordered Cornwallis to halt his pursuit of Washington. Instead, the British seized Newport, Rhode Island, in an amphibious assault by a detachment under Clinton with naval support. Before pulling back most of his forces to winter quarters in New York, Howe established an outpost line in New Jersey between Trenton and Bordentown on the northern bank of the Delaware River, with the line of communications back to the Hudson River and New York guarded by further outposts at Princeton, New Brunswick, and Perth Amboy. Howe could be pleased with his efforts of the year. Despite a late start, the British had seized a base area for operations in the following year, which might not even be needed, as it appeared that the American rebellion was about to collapse.

The Battle of Trenton

South of the Delaware River, Washington knew that a bold stroke was needed. Only a major success would salvage the American position by restoring national

morale and, more important in the short term, boosting enlistment in the Continental Army and persuading its existing soldiers to re-enlist. On the Pennsylvanian side of the Delaware River, Washington's strength was slowly rising as the surviving 2,000 men of Lee's command, eight understrength regiments of the Northern Army, and some Pennsylvania militia units arrived. By the last week in December, Washington could muster about 7,000 men, who would have to be used before their enlistments expired on December 31.

In a move of extraordinary courage, Washington decided to strike the Hessian garrisons of Trenton and Bordentown, which were likely to be at a low state of capability when the attacks were launched on Christmas night. Washington's plan was based on movements by three separate forces. The first was made up of 2,400 men of the Continental Army led by Washington himself, which was to cross the Delaware River nine miles above Trenton at McConkey's Ferry and then advance in two columns to arrive at opposite ends of Trenton's main street early in the morning of December 26. The

The Battle of Trenton on December 26, 1776, was a turning point of the Revolutionary War. Before the battle, the Americans were close to defeat, and the revolution was dying. After the battle, the Americans were revived, and poised on the British line of communication from New York.

General Charles Cornwallis

For further references see pages 56, 58, 59, 60, 65, 95, 98, 102, *103*, 104, 110, 111, 113, 114, 116, *117*, 118, 121, *122*, 124, 125, *126*.

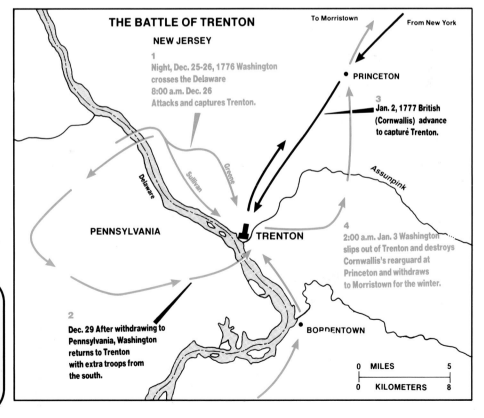

THE BATTLE OF TRENTON
NEW JERSEY

1
Night, Dec. 25-26, 1776 Washington crosses the Delaware
8:00 a.m. Dec. 26
Attacks and captures Trenton.

To Morristown   From New York

• PRINCETON

3
Jan. 2, 1777 British (Cornwallis) advance to capture Trenton.

Assunpink

PENNSYLVANIA

Delaware

Sullivan

Greene

• TRENTON

4
2:00 a.m. Jan. 3 Washington slips out of Trenton and destroys Cornwallis's rearguard at Princeton and withdraws to Morristown for the winter.

2
Dec. 29 After withdrawing to Pennsylvania, Washington returns to Trenton with extra troops from the south.

• BORDENTOWN

0   MILES   5
0   KILOMETERS   8

Washington's planning and execution of the Battle of Trenton remain superb examples of their type of strategy. They also delivered an all-important psychological blow to the British.

second force was to be provided by Pennsylvania militiamen who, under the control of Brigadier General James Ewing, were to cross the Delaware opposite Trenton to cut the garrison's escape route across Assunpink Creek. The third force was also to be made up mainly of militiamen who, under the command of Colonel James Cadwalader, were to cross the Delaware below Bordentown before falling on the garrison.

The night chosen for the attack was cold and windy, and flying snow made visibility very poor. The Delaware was filled with blocks of drifting ice, and neither Ewing's nor Cadwalader's forces were able to cross. But spurred on by the commander-in-chief's total determination, the main force managed to reach the northern bank of the river and divided into the planned two columns under Greene and Sullivan. They reached their planned starting points outside Trenton after Sullivan's column advanced along the river road and Greene's on the inland road.

The Hessian garrison of 1,400 men under Colonel Johann Rall was taken completely by surprise. For the loss of four dead (including two frozen to death) and four wounded, Washington's force killed 40 of the garrison including the commander, and captured 918 more. About 40 Hessians escaped to Bordentown across Assunpink Creek, which should have been held by Ewing's force. The Americans also captured a large quantity of materiel including cannons, small arms, and ammunition of huge importance to the Continental Army.

The Battle of Trenton was a great boost to American morale, reflected strongly in the fact that Washington was then able to persuade many of his men to extend their enlistment by six weeks. The commander used a full appeal to the patriotism of his men, but also had to offer $10 per man in hard money. On the night of December 30-31 Washington again crossed the Delaware and occupied Trenton, this time with about 5,000 men. Cornwallis had been stung by the defeat at Trenton and had responded by calling in his detachments scattered throughout New Jersey to create a force of about 8,000 men. With them he intended to box Washington in

Washington accepts the Hessian surrender after the Battle of Trenton. Particularly important to the American effort was the capture of many small arms and cannon, and other useful equipment and supplies.

between the Delaware and the Atlantic Ocean.

Another British Delay

After a forced march, Cornwallis' initial force of 5,000 troops reached Trenton on January 2, 1777, and took up position outside the town. Cornwallis was sure that he had Washington trapped and postponed the start of his attack to the following day. He hoped that this would allow his men to rest before fighting and give the follow-up force of 2,500 more men the chance to travel the 12 miles from Princeton. Washington had 5,200 men, but was becoming increasingly worried about the reliability of the 3,600 militiamen among them. During that night, therefore, the Americans slipped away to the east along the disused old road to Princeton, deceiving the British by leaving their camp fires burning.

On January 3, Washington fell on the British regiments that were just leaving Princeton to reinforce Cornwallis and in

the Battle of Princeton inflicted heavy losses on them. On hearing the news of this latest reverse Cornwallis became increasingly worried about his comparatively long and vulnerable lines of communication. He decided not to pursue Washington as the latter led his men toward Morristown, but instead made for winter quarters at New Brunswick and Perth Amboy at the mouth of the Raritan River. Washington had achieved what he had intended, and his forces established their own winter quarters in the hills around Morristown.

In a period of 10 days, Washington, "fanning dying embers into a lively flame," had put new heart into the American Revolution and its war for independence. Frederick the Great of Prussia, one of the few undisputed "great captains," said that Washington's Trenton campaign was one of the most brilliant campaigns in history. The American victories at Trenton and Princeton were in themselves comparatively small, but they meant that Washington would have an army for the new year's campaigning season. On the other side, Cornwallis' withdrawal to the Raritan meant that Howe's base area was reduced from a viable launch point for next year's offensive to just the city of New York, a foothold in New Jersey and the port of Newport.

Those Americans with political and strategic sense now knew that throwing off British rule would be no easy matter, and Washington remained more than ever convinced that his best course was maintaining the Continental Army without risking battle in order to eventually wear down the British. The British were currently faced with a great strategic problem: for they had to put down the rebellion so crushingly that the French would not dare to enter the war openly on the side of the Americans. So 1777 was the year in which the British could make or break the American Revolution, and this fact should have been reflected in a tight strategy under a single commander. In fact it was the year in which British planning was most confused and the resulting operations least coordinated.

Britain's Only Coherent Plan of the War

As early as November 30, 1776, Howe had put forward an overall plan that was the most far-sighted and comprehensive devised by any British commander during the war. From his base area in New York, New Jersey and Rhode Island, Howe planned an early start to the campaigning season such as he had been denied earlier in the year. Howe's plan was to leave garrisons totaling 15,000 men (8,000 in New Jersey to check Washington and 7,000 as garrison of New York), while using the rest of his army for offensive operations. One force of 10,000 men was to be launched from Newport into New England while a second force of 10,000 men would advance up the Hudson River to meet a British force advancing from Quebec via Lake Champlain. Assuming that these spring and summer moves were successful, Howe proposed to take Philadelphia in the fall and then advance

The death of Brigadier General Mercer in the Battle of Princeton on January 3, 1777. The battle was small, but fought with great determination, and it had important strategic consequences.

Washington's headquarters during the winter of 1777. After victory at Princeton the American army went into winter quarters at Morristown, New Jersey.

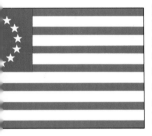

The first Stars and Stripes which was adopted by the Continental Congress, 14 June, 1777.

into the southern states during the winter. Howe estimated that he needed 35,000 men for the year's campaign, yet he had only 20,000 men in America. The request for 15,000 more men went to London, which countered with an offer of 8,000 men. But even before he received London's answer, Howe had begun to alter his plan in the light of Washington's successes in New Jersey and now planned to make Philadelphia the main objective of his 1777 campaign. On March 3, 1777 this revised plan was approved in London, together with a reinforcement of 5,500 men and the suggestion that Howe launch a diversionary move in New England. Meanwhile Burgoyne had succeeded in having the Quebec command made independent of Howe, so creating the dangerous situation of divided commands in North America. Burgoyne proposed that his forces should advance south to link up with those of Howe. This plan was approved in London on March 29, though no real thought was given to exactly how Burgoyne and Howe should link up. The only two possibilities were a junction of Burgoyne's advance and Howe's New England diversion, or an early success against Philadelphia by Howe so that he could return to New York and then advance north. The British thus entered the campaigning season of 1777 with two commanders and two strategic plans. Even when he learned on August 3 that he could expect no cooperation from Howe, the ambitious Burgoyne refused to alter his own scheme.

The need to have these plans confirmed in London combined with delays in the arrival of reinforcements and supplies meant that many of the campaigning season's earlier months were lost. The sole episode of note was a raid on April 25 launched under Major General William Tryon, British governor of New York. This attack destroyed the American depot at Danbury, Connecticut but was then harried all the way back to the British lines by a militia force under Arnold.

Support From the French

The British loss of time was Washington's gain. Men to form the new Continental Army were arriving slowly. It was June before Washington could call on 8,000 men in New Jersey, and the Northern Army was in an even poorer state. The situation was made worse still by a lack of all types of equipment, food, and even clothing. All were in desperately short supply until the secret arrival of three French ships. They carried many of the items which the Americans could not produce for themselves. An American mission in France was meanwhile working to bring France into the war as an open ally of the Continentals. The French agreed in principle, but decided to wait until the Americans proved their determination and capability with a major victory. With the foreign supplies, a number of

The Marquis de Lafayette occupies a special place in American military history as the Frenchman who arrived in a time of crisis to offer practical help. It is therefore not surprising, that Americans serving in the French Air Force before the United States entered into World War I were grouped into a unit known as the "Lafayette Escadrille."

European officers began to arrive. Many were adventurers of little real skill, especially in the high ranks they demanded, but they could offer the knowledge of professional soldiers. Among them were several who proved very important to the Continental Army: Louis Du Portail and Thaddeus Kosciuszko were experienced engineers and skilled teachers; Casimir Pulaski raised the Continental Army's first effective cavalry unit; Johann de Kalb and Marie Joseph du Motier le Marquis de Lafayette became good leaders as well as excellent practical teachers; and Friedrich Wilhelm von Steuben proved a superb trainer of men.

Washington Evades the British

Howe spent June 1777 in a series of maneuvers designed to coax Washington into battle before the British commander launched his main offensive toward Philadelphia. Washington's army was based at Middlebrook, New Jersey, so that the American commander-in-chief could respond to a British move southwest against Philadelphia or north up the Hudson River. Washington was not to be tempted, however, for he knew he must avoid battle to keep his army intact. Yet he also understood the importance of keep-

Marquis de Lafayette
For further references see pages 82, *86*, 115, *116*, 117, 121, 122, 124.

Gunner, Hesse-Kassel Artillery Company (1776)

Hesse-Kassel sent three companies of artillery (two of them specially raised for the purpose) to serve with the British in America, and this was the German state's complete corps of artillery. The three companies arrived on Long Island in 1776, and took part in nearly every major engagement of the Revolutionary War. Each company was made up of five officers, 14 non-commissioned officers, three drummers and 129 gunners, and the weapon used was mainly the light 4-pounder field gun. The gunner's uniform was similar to that of most artillerymen except that the facings were nearer crimson than scarlet, and the vest and breeches were a yellow-buff color.

THE STARS AND STRIPES·
WASHINGTON DESCRIBING THE FLAG TO LAFAYETTE
AND OTHER FRENCH AND AMERICAN OFFICERS

We got the stars from Heaven
The Red from our Mother Country
Separating it with White stripes
Thus showing that we have
Separated from her
And the White stripes shall
Go down to Posterity representing
LIBERTY" G...

ing at least some of his forces in front of the British. American senior officers generally agreed with Washington that the main British effort would take place on the Hudson River/Lake Champlain line, probably in the form of an advance to the north by Howe and to the south by Burgoyne. Washington detached part of his force under Putnam to garrison four forts on the west bank of the Hudson River between 30 and 40 miles north of New York, and later he detached another small force to aid the Northern Army against Burgoyne's advance.

Washington kept the bulk of his army ready to intercept any movement by Howe's forces directly toward Philadelphia, the American capital which was protected by a series of forts along the Delaware River and by obstacles to the sea approaches. For two months, Howe kept up his effort to tempt Washington into a pitched battle. Then he switched plans. On August 23 he embarked 18,000 soldiers on transports for the short voyage into Chesapeake Bay, where the troops were landed on August 25 at Head of Elk (now Elkton) on the Elk River. This effective use of sea power put the British in the Americans' rear, and on the correct side of the Delaware River for an overland advance to Philadelphia. Washington rapidly moved south with 10,500 men to take up a defensive position on the east bank of Brandywine Creek, barring the British move on Philadelphia.

The Battle of the Brandywine

The American forward positions at Cooch's Bridge were swept aside on September 2 by the advance of Howe's main force. The British then pushed forward to the Americans' main position on the Brandywine between Chad's Ford and a point opposite Parkerville. On September 11, the Battle of the Brandywine was fought. Washington had deployed his army well forward in two parts, the left wing under his own command and the right wing under Sullivan. Howe repeated the tactic that had proved successful on Long Island: the British right, in the form of General Wilhelm von Knyphausen's Hessian contingent, demonstrated in front of the American left while Cornwallis took the British left on a long march to the ford at Sconneltown above the American right

George Washington shows the Stars and Stripes to the Marquis de Lafayette and other French and American officers. Adopted by the Continental Congress on June 14, 1777, this flag was composed of seven red stripes separated by six white stripes and, in the field, a blue rectangle containing a circlet of 13 white stars, one for each new state.

The Chew House was the key to the Battle of Germantown on October 4, 1777. The advancing American columns were checked by concentrated British fire from the house, which had been turned into an effective strongpoint.

flank. Lacking cavalry for reconnaissance Sullivan learned of Cornwallis' approach only at the last minute and was caught as he tried to change fronts to meet the British attack. Sullivan's wing broke in disorder, and Cornwallis' men advanced to cut Washington's line of retreat at Dilworth. The American commander sent Greene with two brigades to check this threatening move, weakening his own front so much that he had to retreat before the Hessian advance. But Greene's effort had saved the Continental Army, which pulled back to Chester after losing 1,000 men; the British lost 526 men.

Howe moved skillfully forward to Philadelphia in a series of pinning and flanking movements, and the way was finally cleared on September 21 when a British night attack on Paoli routed Brigadier General Anthony Wayne's brigade. Philadelphia was quickly evacuated, and the Continental Congress moved first to Lancaster and then to York as once more it decreed dictatorial powers for Washington. The British entered Philadelphia on September 26. Only after combined army and navy operations between October 22 and November 20 did they overcome the stubborn resistance of Forts Mifflin and Mercer lower down the

Delaware. Then the British could ship reinforcements and supplies into the captured American capital.

The British Occupation of Philadelphia

Once in Philadelphia, Howe dispersed his forces slightly. Retaining his main strength in the city, he deployed 9,000 men in Germantown north of Philadelphia and another 3,000 in New Jersey, thereby securing his overland line of communications with New York. Just as Howe had repeated his Long Island tactic at the Brandywine, Washington now tried to win a victory with an adaptation of his Trenton tactic, in this instance against the Germantown garrison. Trenton had involved the movement of only two columns of men over short distances. Washington's Germantown plan was on a larger scale involving 13,000 men. The plan called for a converging advance by four columns, two of militiamen on the flanks and two of the Continental Army (commanded on the left by Greene and on the right by Sullivan) on four roads to meet in Germantown at dawn on October 4. The Battle of Germantown was an American

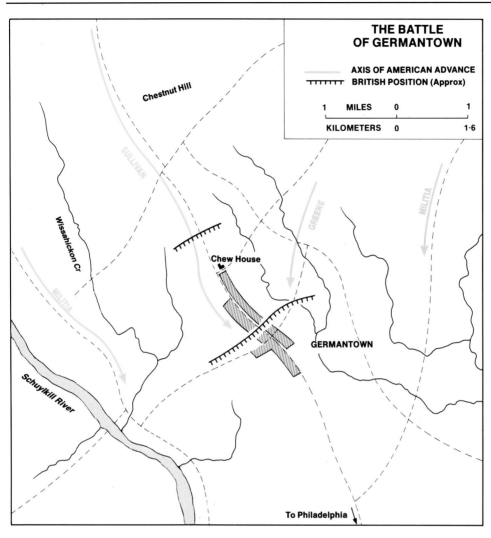

THE BATTLE
OF GERMANTOWN

——— AXIS OF AMERICAN ADVANCE
ттттттт BRITISH POSITION (Approx)

1   MILES   0   1
KILOMETERS   0   1·6

Chestnut Hill

SULLIVAN

Wissahickon Cr

MILITIA

GREENE

MILITIA

Chew House

GERMANTOWN

Schuylkill River

To Philadelphia

The Battle of Germantown on October 4, 1777, revealed to Washington with great clarity the problems faced by a commander who divided his command into four separate columns, especially when two of them were made up mainly of inexperienced militiamen.

failure: the two militia columns never arrived, and the two Continental Army columns fired on each other as they approached Germantown. The British fell back before Sullivan's column, but left a detachment of sharpshooters in the stone Chew House. The two American generals spent so much time arguing whether or not to take the house that the British had time to re-form and advance, forcing the Americans to retreat after suffering 700 casualties and losing 400 men captured.

Howe brought his army together after Germantown and moved forward to tackle Washington at Whitemarsh. But the British commander then pulled his army back into winter quarters in Philadelphia without forcing a battle, leaving Washington to choose his own winter quarters at Valley Forge, about 20 miles northwest of Philadelphia.

Burgoyne's Invasion of New York

Howe's offensive can only be regarded as ponderous, and it was ultimately of less importance than the other British effort of the year. This was Burgoyne's northern operation, which also began in June 1777 with Albany, New York, as its first objective. Burgoyne divided his command into two parts. At the head of the larger force made up of 7,200 regulars (4,000 British and 3,200 Hessian) supported by 650 loyalists, Canadians, and Indians, Burgoyne was to advance up the Richelieu River, through Lake Champlain, and past Lake George to take Saratoga before advancing on Albany just below the point where the Mohawk River flows into the Hudson River. At the head of the smaller unit of 700 regular troops sup-

Major General Sir John Burgoyne commanded the British forces in Canada. He failed to establish effective coordination of his operations with those of Sir John Howe farther to the south.

ported by 175 loyalists under Sir John Johnson and about 1,000 Iroquois under Thayendanega, also known as Joseph Brant, Lieutenant Colonel Barry St. Leger was to move up the St. Lawrence River and through Lake Ontario to Fort Oswego. From here, he was to advance up the river to Lake Oneida before striking cross-country to the headwaters of the Mohawk River at Fort Stanwix, also known as Fort Schuyler (now Rome), and then advancing down the river to link up with Burgoyne at Albany.

On paper the plan looked workable, but in practice it ignored all the problems of divided commands seeking to meet at a common objective without any effective means of communication between the two forces. Burgoyne reduced his chances still further by forgetting the hard-learned lessons of the French and Indian War and starting a wilderness campaign with 138 pieces of artillery, an enormous amount of baggage and a large number of women.

Burgoyne's progress as far as the southern end of Lake Champlain was completed without difficulty, for the Northern Army under Schuyler mustered only 2,950 men (2,500 at Ticonderoga and 450 at Fort Stanwix). The problems of Schuyler, a New Yorker of aristocratic manner, were made worse by the fact that the New Englanders in his army generally refused to obey his orders and indeed openly argued for replacement of Schuyler by Gates. Inevitably the Americans were unable to offer any effective resistance to Burgoyne, who arrived outside Fort Ticonderoga on July 1 and soon emplaced his artillery on a height overlooking the fort. Brigadier General Arthur St. Clair saw that resistance would serve no purpose but to cost the Americans casualties they could not replace, and on the night of July 5-6, he evacuated the fort and retreated southeast into Vermont, while sending the sick and wounded and his command's baggage by boat south to Skenesborough (now Whitehall).

Burgoyne immediately launched a pursuit, his advance guard by road and the main body by water. Burgoyne overtook the American rearguard on July 7, and in the Battle of Hubbardton, decisively crushed it. The fighting stand of Seth

Warner's militia detachment bought enough time for St. Clair to slip away via Rutland to link up with Schuyler at Fort Edward on the upper Hudson north of Saratoga. St. Clair's baggage train was captured at Skenesborough. Burgoyne now decided to deviate from his original plan, which had called for the British army to be floated down Lake George, and instead decided on an overland advance from Skenesborough toward Saratoga, though the heavy equipment still had to use the Lake George route.

American "Scorched Earth" Policy

As they pulled back, the Americans devastated the region's already rough roads, destroyed the bridges over numerous deep ravines, felled trees onto the road and dug ditches to flood dry ground with swamp water. The efforts were aided by torrential rain that swelled creeks and turned dirt into thick mud. It took Burgoyne three weeks to reach Fort Edward, where on July 29 he found that Schuyler had pulled back to Stillwater. American strength was now increasing, though still not to the point at which Schuyler could seriously contemplate giving battle to a considerably weakened Burgoyne. Washington sent

Daniel Morgan, who rose to the rank of brigadier general, was one of several Americans who showed great tactical skill in the Revolutionary War. He was also the officer largely responsible for proving that riflemen could be very effective in spite of the slow rate of their fire.

Major Generals Arnold and Benjamin Lincoln to support Schuyler, the latter a Massachusetts officer possessing considerable influence over the New Englanders who were still a thorn in Schuyler's side. Schuyler was also bolstered by the arrival of 1,600 militiamen, as well as 3,000 men of the Continental Army, including 500 men of Colonel Daniel Morgan's rifle regiment and 750 men supplied by Putnam in New York.

Schuyler's most important new strength was the manpower of the local militia units, which had become increasingly angry with the terrorization of their home areas by Burgoyne's virtually uncontrolled Indians. The single most important event was the murder and scalping of Jane McCrea, after which many more men came forward for militia service. These units still refused to serve under Schuyler, and command of these units was therefore entrusted to John Stark, who was commissioned as a brigadier general by New Hampshire. Stark raised a 2,000-man force and took up position at Bennington in southern Vermont to block any advance which may be planned by Burgoyne into New England and thus on to further secure positions.

Private, Morgan's Rifle Corps (1777)

Volunteers from the frontier of Virginia, the men of Morgan's Rifle Corps were extremely capable skirmishers and scouts, and also proved themselves notably self-reliant and used their own Pennsylvania rifles, powder horns and leather bullet bags. The fringed hunting shirt and trousers were made of white linen.

Burgoyne Checked at Saratoga

As the Americans grew in strength, Burgoyne learned on August 3 that Howe would not be making any northern diversion that could lead to a link-up of two major British forces. By now the British were very short of supplies and all types of transportation, and on August 11, Burgoyne ordered Colonel Friedrich Baum to take 650 Brunswickers to forage in the Bennington area. On August 16 the German force was surrounded and destroyed by Stark's force in the Battle of Bennington. Arriving later in the same day to reinforce Baum, the 650 Brunswickers of Colonel Heidrich von Breymann were in turn destroyed. Von Breymann escaped with less than two-thirds of his men. The American militiamen, supported by Warner's "Green Mountain Boys" after a forced march from Manchester, suffered only 70 casualties (30 dead and 40 wounded), but killed 207 of the enemy and captured another 700. The Americans also captured a useful quantity of small arms, light artillery, and wagons. It was an important reverse for Burgoyne, who was deprived not only of much needed food and transportation, but also, about one-tenth of his strength.

Like that of Burgoyne, St. Leger's initial movement had been completed without difficulty, and the combined British, German, loyalist and Iroquois force assembled at Fort Oswego on July 25. St. Leger then moved up the Oswego River to Lake Oneida, continued by water to the eastern end of the lake, and struck out overland again to Fort Stanwix. The British force arrived on August 2 and on the following day laid siege to the American garrison, whose men decided to hold out to the bitter end as they anticipated an Indian massacre if they tried to retreat.

The Battle of Fort Stanwix

As soon as news of the British siege reached him on August 4, Brigadier General Nicholas Herkimer of the Tryon County militia set off with a relief force of 800 local militiamen. On August 6 the relief

Burgoyne sent two Hessian columns to invade Vermont. American militia gathered under popular leaders such as John Stock to resist the Hessians. The Militia defeated and captured the Hessians at the Battle of Bennington, 16th August, 1777. An American Militia man recalls the battle.

''I enlisted at Francestown, N.H., in Colonel Stickney's regiment and Captain Clark's company, as soon as I learned that Stark would accept the command of the State troops; six or seven others from the same town joined the army at the same time. We marched forthwith to Number Four, and stayed there a week. Meantime I received a horn of powder and run two or three hundred bullets; I had brought my own gun. Then my company went on to Manchester; soon after I went, with a hundred others, under Colonel Emerson, down the valley of Otter Creek; on this excursion we lived like lords, on pigs and chickens, in the houses of tories who had fled. When we returned to Manchester, bringing two hogsheads of West India rum, we heard that the Hessians were on their way to invade Vermont. Late in the afternoon of rainy Friday, we were ordered off for Bennington in spite of rain, mud and darkness. We pushed on all night, making the best progress we could; about day-break I, with Lieut. Miltimore, came near Bennington, and slept a little while on a hay-mow, when the barn-yard fowls waked us; we went for bread and milk to the sign of the 'wolf,' and then hurried three miles west to Stark's main body.

Stark and ****** rode up near the enemy to reconnoitre; were fired at by the cannon, and came galloping back. Stark rode with shoulders bent forward, and cried out to his men: 'Those rascals know that I am an officer; don't you see they honor me with a big gun as a salute.' We were marched round and round a circular hill till we were tired. Stark said it was to amuse the Germans. All the while a cannonade was kept up upon us from their breast-works; it hurst no body, and it lessened our fear of the great guns. After a while I was sent, with twelve others, to lie in ambush, on a knoll a little north, and watch for tories on their way to join Baum. Presently we saw six coming toward us who, mistrusting us for tories, came too near us to escape. We disarmed and sent them, under a guard of three, to Stark.

Between two and three o'clock the battle began. The Germans fired by platoons, and were soon hidden by the smoke. Our men fired each on his own hook, aiming wherever he saw a flash; few on our side had either bayonets or cartridges. At last I stole away from my post and ran down to the battle. The first time I fired I put three balls in my gun; before I had time to fire many rounds our men rushed over the breast-works, but I and many others chased straggling Hessians in the woods; we pursued until we met Breyman with 800 fresh troops and larger cannon, which opened a fire of grape shot; some of the grape shot riddled a Virginia fence near me; one shot struck a small white oak behind which I stood; though it hit higher than my head I fled from the tree, thinking it might be aimed at again. We skirmishers ran back till we met a large body of Stark's men and then faced about. I soon started for a brook I saw a few rods behind, for I had drank and forgot my thirst. But the enemy outflanked us, and I said to a comrade, 'we must run, or they will have us.' He said: 'I will have one fire first.' At that moment, a major, on a black horse, rode along behind us, shouting 'fight on boys, reinforcements close by.' While he was yet speaking, a grape shot went through his horse's head; it bled a good deal, but the major kept his seat, and rode on to encourage others. In a few minutes we saw Warner's men hurrying to help us; they opened right and left of us, and one half of them attacked each flank of the enemy, and beat back those who were just closing round us. Stark's men now took heart and stood their ground. My gun barrel was at this time too hot to hold, so I seized the musket of a dead Hessian, in which my bullets went down easier than in my own. Right in front were the cannon, and seeing an officer on horse-back waving his sword to the artillery, I fired at him twice; his horse fell; he cut the traces of an artillery horse, mounted him and rode off. I afterward heard that the officer was Major Skene. Soon the Germans ran, and we followed; many of them threw down their guns on the ground, or offered them to us, or kneeled, some in puddles of water. One said to me, 'Wir sind ein bruder!' I pushed him behind me and rushed on. The enemy beat a parley, minded to give up, but our men did not understand it. I came to one wounded man flat on the ground, crying water or quarter. I snatched the sword out of his scabbard, and while I ran on and fired, carried it in my mouth, thinking I might need it. The Germans fled by the road and in a wood each side of it; many of their scabbards caught in the brush and held the fugitives till we seized them. We chased them till dark, Colonel Johnston, of Haverhill, wanted to chase them all night. We might have mastered them all, as they stopped within three miles of the battle field; but Stark, saying 'he would run no risk of spoiling a good day's work, ordered a halt, and return to quarters.

I was coming back, when I was ordered by Stark himself, who knew me, as I had been one of his body gaurds in Canada, to help draw off a field-piece. I told him 'I was worn out.' his answer was, 'don't seem to disobey; take hold, and if you can't hold out, slip away in the dark.' Before we had dragged the gun far, Warner rode near us. Some one pointing to a dead man by the road- side, said, 'Your brother is killed', 'Is it Jesse?' asked Warner. And when the answer was 'yes', he jumped off his horse, stooped and gazed in the dead man's face, and then rode away without saying a word.''

force was ambushed by the Iroquois in a wooded ravine near Oriskany about 6 miles from Fort Stanwix, and after a bloody battle fought during a thunderstorm, the mortally wounded Herkimer ordered the remnants of his command to scatter into the woods. Casualties were heavy on both sides, and while the loss of nearly half their strength meant that the militiamen could not relieve Fort Stanwix, their own losses further worried the Indians, who were already unhappy with the static nature of the Fort Stanwix operation. Insult was added to injury as the garrison made a sortie during the Battle of Oriskany and devastated St. Leger's camp.

Despite the fact that Burgoyne was only 24 miles away from his position at Stillwater, Schuyler decided that Fort Stanwix had to be relieved and allowed the detachment of 950 Continental Army volunteers under Arnold, who moved as rapidly as possible up the Mohawk River, to set out. Arnold cleverly sent ahead a half-witted Dutchman, his clothes full of

holes, together with an Oneida Indian guide, to tell the Iroquois that the Continental Army was advancing "as numerous as the leaves on the trees." Believing that such a man could only be telling the truth, the Iroquois decamped after scalping a number of loyalists. This left St. Leger seriously exposed, and on August 22, the British commander abandoned the siege, and his camp, to fall back to Fort Oswego leaving the Americans his artillery and supplies.

Early in September, the news of St. Leger's failure reached Burgoyne, who now understood that he would receive help from neither Howe nor St. Leger. Burgoyne's report to London provides a telling indication of the strengths of the Americans: "The great bulk of the country is undoubtedly with Congress in principle and zeal; and their measures are executed with a secrecy and dispatch that are not to be equalled. Wherever the King's forces point, militia in the amount of three or four thousand assemble in twenty-four hours; they bring with them their subsi-

The Battle of Bennington on August 16, 1777, was a major tactical success for the Americans. In the battle, the "Green Mountain Boys" deprived the British of about one-tenth of their overall strength and, by destroying and capturing much of their wheeled transport, effectively removed from them any real chance of living off the land.

Burgoyne meets with his Indian allies at Saratoga. The Indians provided the British with an effective capability for skirmishing and reconnaissance. But reports of their atrocities so inflamed local Americans that many joined the Continental Army under Gates.

stence, etc., and the alarm over, they return to their farms..."

Burgoyne's Fatal Gamble

But Burgoyne was not deterred from pushing forward, and having occupied Saratoga he now gambled on reaching Albany or losing his army. Despite the fact that the increasing number of deserters from his Indian allies had left him with no effective means of gathering tactical intelligence, Burgoyne crossed to the western bank of the Hudson River on September 13 and prepared to advance along the riverbank road. The British commander also sent a request for aid to Clinton in New York. On August 19, the Continental Congress had at last yielded to New England pressure and replaced Schuyler with Gates. Gates was a clever commander who fully understood Burgoyne's problems. He therefore advanced four miles from Schuyler's Stillwater position to the Bemis Heights, where the technical skills of Brigadier General Kosciuszko created an entrenched position around Neilson's Barn to command the riverbank road.

The 1st Battle of Saratoga, or the Battle of Freeman's Farm, took place on September 19. Advancing with 6,000 men against 7,000, Burgoyne saw that a frontal effort could stand little chance. Therefore, he detached 4,200 men in three columns commanded by von Riedesel, Hamilton, and Fraser in an attempt to outflank the Americans' left with a turning movement past Freeman's Farm. Gates detached 3,000 of his men under Arnold to deal with this British attack, which was beaten back. Particular damage was done by the riflemen under Morgan. After suffering 600 casualties to the Americans' 300 the British halted. Arnold asked Gates for reinforcements so that he could counterattack, but Gates refused, and the lines of the two armies stabilized. For the next three weeks, skirmishing occurred as the British dug in and waited for the help promised by Clinton.

Its arrival amounted to no more than a gesture. With a force of only 7,000 men available to him in the New York area, Clinton advanced with 4,000 men up the Hudson River and on October 4 stormed Forts Clinton and Montgomery in the New York highlands. Clinton was a cautious commander and was now satisfied that his effort had materially aided Burgoyne. Sending his advance guard farther forward by ship to burn Esopus (now Kingston), Clinton pulled back to New York. Burgoyne was on his own and now had to prepare to face Gates.

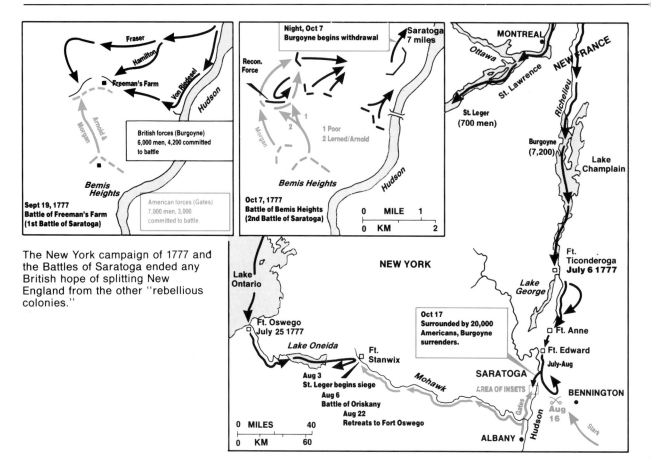

The New York campaign of 1777 and the Battles of Saratoga ended any British hope of splitting New England from the other "rebellious colonies."

Map labels (left inset):

Fraser
Hamilton
Freeman's Farm
Von Riedesel
Hudson
Arnold & Morgan
Bemis Heights

British forces (Burgoyne) 6,000 men, 4,200 committed to battle

American forces (Gates) 7,000 men, 3,000 committed to battle.

Sept 19, 1777 Battle of Freeman's Farm (1st Battle of Saratoga)

Map labels (center inset):

Night, Oct 7 Burgoyne begins withdrawal
Saratoga 7 miles
Recon. Force
Morgan
1 Poor
2 Lerned/Arnold
Bemis Heights
Hudson
Oct 7, 1777 Battle of Bemis Heights (2nd Battle of Saratoga)

0   MILE   1
0   KM   2

Map labels (right):

MONTREAL
Ottawa
St. Lawrence
NEW FRANCE
St. Leger (700 men)
Richelieu
Burgoyne (7,200)
Lake Champlain
Ft. Ticonderoga July 6 1777
NEW YORK
Lake George
Ft. Anne
Ft. Edward July-Aug
Lake Ontario
Ft. Oswego July 25 1777
Lake Oneida
Ft. Stanwix
Aug 3 St. Leger begins siege
Aug 6 Battle of Oriskany
Aug 22 Retreats to Fort Oswego
Mohawk
Oct 17 Surrounded by 20,000 Americans, Burgoyne surrenders.
SARATOGA
AREA OF INSETS
Gates
BENNINGTON
Aug 16
Stark
Hudson
ALBANY

0   MILES   40
0   KM   60

The Second Battle of Saratoga

Gates knew that he had only to wait. The British had to try to break through to Albany as they were desperately short of all supplies, food was running out, the animals had exhausted all possible grazing, and desertion was becoming an acute problem. Meanwhile, American strength was increasing as militia units continued to arrive. By October 7, Gates had more than 10,000 men under his command. On this day, Burgoyne sent out a "reconnaissance in force" to test the American position and hopefully to turn the Americans' left flank. So the Second Battle of Saratoga, otherwise known as the Battle of Bemis Heights began. Gates responded to the British "reconnaissance in force" by dispatching a force containing Morgan's riflemen. They drove the British back to their fortified position. Arnold had been at loggerheads with Gates and was confined to his tent, but he could not sit idly while the battles were being fought.

Above: A British cartoon summarizes the feeling in Great Britain when news of Burgoyne's surrender at Saratoga arrived.

Left: Severe fighting was the order of the day on and around the earthworks in the Second Battle of Saratoga (the Battle of Bemis Heights) October 7, 1777.

Arnold rushed out to take part in the American counterattack and was wounded in the attack on Breymann's Redoubt. By nightfall, the British had been forced back to their defense line on the river, having suffered 600 casualties to the Americans' 150.

With only 5,700 men left, Burgoyne fell back toward Saratoga two days later. The American militia worked their way around the British flanks and cut Burgoyne's already inadequate supply lines. Faced with more than 18,000 better supplied Americans who were in a superior position, Burgoyne had no alternative but to surrender on October 17. All his men passed into captivity, and large quantities of arms, ammunition and yet more supplies fell into American hands. The ''Convention of Saratoga'' established that the disarmed British soldiers should be marched to Boston for evacuation under parole to Great Britain. In a shameful repudiation of these terms, the Continental Congress later decided that the prisoners should not be allowed to return home.

The surrender of General Burgoyne at Saratoga on October 16, 1777. This was a major blow to British plans for the defeat of the American ''rebellion.''

Private, Pennsylvania State Regiment (1777)

State troops were organized for defense of their parent states and were not part of the Continental Army or the state militia. By the early part of 1777, Pennsylvania possessed, in addition to units of Continental service, a state artillery regiment and a state infantry regiment. These were taken into Continental service in June and November 1777 respectively. The Pennsylvania State Regiment contained both rifle and musket men, the latter wearing blue coats with red or white facings depending on cloth availability when the coat was made. A blanket roll was often carried in place of a regular knapsack.

Turning Point in the Revolutionary War

The American victory at Saratoga was a major turning point of the Revolutionary War. For the Americans this triumph more than balanced the failure of Washington against Howe. As for the British, the failure of Burgoyne meant that their positions in America had to be reviewed, with the result that Ticonderoga and Crown Point were abandoned to leave the British in control only of New York, Philadelphia and part of Rhode Island. Most important of all, it persuaded France to recognize the United States. On February 6, 1778, a Franco-American alliance was sealed by the signature of two agreements. The first was a treaty of friendship and commerce, the other a military alliance to become effective if and when war broke out between France and Great Britain.

The Ordeal at Valley Forge

This, however, was in the future. The ordeal of the Continental Army at Valley Forge during the savage winter of 1777-78 still had to be faced.

Valley Forge has since become a symbol of patriotic suffering, bravery, and endurance. When Washington retired to winter quarters at Valley Forge during October 1777, he had with him the 6,000-man core of the Continental Army. At first, the men had only tattered tents with which to keep at bay the increasingly bitter wind. At the beginning of the Valley Forge winter, some men lacked blankets shoes, and even pants. As the snows came, the supply position became much more difficult: for weeks, there was no meat. The men were at times forced to boil shoes and eat the only slightly softened leather.

It was not that there were no supplies, in various depots spoiled food, and clothing was unissued. The problem lay with the failure of the Continental supply system, which had been hamstrung since mid-1777 by the resignations of the quartermaster general and commissary general, who saw that there was more money to be made in civilian life than in the army. Established in York, Pennsylvania, the Continental Congress was split by factional intrigue and could not appoint men to either of these immensely important posts. The result was that the existing supply services tried, but only half-heartedly, to resolve the physical difficulties of supplying the army at Valley Forge, and in the process caused their own men immense hardship. The position was complicated by the activities of the Conway cabal, which from September 25, 1777, tried to oust Washington from supreme command in favor of Gates. In 1777, Gates was appointed president of the new Board of War, which numbered among its members at least two enemies of Washington. The leader of the movement to oust Washington was Colonel Thomas Conway, an Irish mercenary who had left French service to join the American cause. Conway had many American supporters in his

The Continental Army's ordeal at Valley Forge was caused not so much by a lack of supplies as by the difficulty of obtaining available supplies out of the bureaucratic system and then moving them with inadequate transportation.

effort to elevate Gates over Washington, but when Conway was unsuccessful and resigned on December 23, the scale of the attack on Washington quickly declined.

From the ordeal of Valley Forge, there emerged a more effective army. Washington persuaded his ablest lieutenant to accept the position of quartermaster general. From then on, the supply situation of the Continental Army improved quite considerably.

Top left: Washington explains matters to a Congressional committee at Valley Forge. By then, the winter had become so bitter than the soldiers had built a virtual town of log cabins to replace their tents.
Above: Only after his men had built their log cabins did Washington occupy this house as his headquarters.
Left: Von Steuben at Valley Forge, where his moves toward true discipline began to create an effective Continental Army.

Von Steuben Revives the Continental Army

Another event of major importance at Valley Forge was the appearance in February 1778 of von Steuben. He claimed to have been created a baron for services to a small German state and to have been a lieutenant general on the staff of Frederick the Great. In reality von Steuben had been only a captain, but he was well versed in the military discipline of the Prussian army. Washington had long wanted to improve the discipline of the Continental Army, and in von Steuben he had the man to achieve this task. Appointed inspector general in charge of training, von Steuben proved to be a superb trainer of men, and one who never failed to know the difference between the American volunteer soldier and the European professional soldier. Von Steuben's training program in the late winter and early spring of 1778 was geared exactly to combining the needs of the Continental Army and the capabilities of the American soldier. Officers were taught the responsibility of looking after their men. The men were drilled in a simplified version of the complex formations and movements of European armies, the care of their equipment, and the effective use of the bayonet. Von Steuben also convinced

the Americans of the importance of light infantry. The first steps to creating such troops for scouting and skirmishing were taken under the German's inspiration. After von Steuben's training program the American soldier was increasingly a match for the British soldier on the open field of battle.

Even as spring began and von Steuben forged ahead with his training program, Howe remained inactive and so lost his last real chance of catching and defeating Washington. Howe was weary of the war and asked to be replaced. His successor was Clinton. As Washington began to prepare for the emergence of the Continental Army from Valley Forge, Clinton was preparing the British evacuation of the American capital in accordance with orders he had received from London. With a French involvement on the side of the Americans becoming inevitable, the British had to consider the defense of their other possessions in the western hemisphere. This was the main reason for Clinton's retirement to New York after the detachment of 5,000 men to the West Indies and 3,000 more to Florida. In New York, Clinton was to consolidate his forces for a vigorous summer offensive. Because he lacked the ships to move 3,000 horses as well as his men, Clinton decided to take the overland route to New York. On June 18, Clinton's army left Philadelphia,

Above: Washington in prayer at Valley Forge.
Above left: Washington at Valley Forge, where the men of the Continental Army endured terrible hardship.

the Americans - somewhat unexpectedly - made contact with the British rear guard Clinton reacted with more speed than Lee, maneuvering to envelop the American right. Lee pulled his force back in circumstances that soon became very confused. This retreat angered Washington. The American commander-in-chief assumed personal command in what had now become a defense against a powerful British counterattack. Both armies became fully involved in this Battle of Monmouth Court House. It lasted until nightfall as a stalemate in which the Americans for the first time matched the British in battlefield skills. Each side admitted to 350 casualties, but the losses

Left: Frederick William Augustus von Steuben, the ex-Prussian army officer who became the Continental Army's disciplinarian task master.
Below: Washington took personal command in the Battle of Monmouth Court House.
Bottom: ''The Heroine of Monmouth'' was Molly Pitcher, who took her dead husband's place at an American cannon and served throughout the battle.

which was immediately reoccupied by Washington.

Washington then followed in the tracks of the British with his full strength of 12,000 and looked for an opportunity to bring Clinton to battle under favorable circumstances. How to do this presented problems. None of Washington's subordinate generals supported a general action. Wayne and de Lafayette suggested a partial attack to tackle a portion of the British army as it straggled in a long column along the road, while the same Lee who had been captured at Morristown (but later exchanged in a swap of prisoners) thought that the best course would be guerrilla action to harass the British.

The Battle of Monmouth Court House

On June 26 Washington settled on a bold approach and decided to launch his advance guard against the rear of the British column once Clinton had set off from his overnight halt at Monmouth Court House on June 27. Command was initially entrusted to de Lafayette, but Lee successfully demanded the command when he learned how large the American force was to be. Lee's advance took American force over rough, unreconnoitered ground. When

Major General Charles Lee must have been a man of odd appearance, for many acquaintances said that this contemporary caricature was, in fact, a good likeness.

Admiral Jean Baptiste le Comte d'Estaing
For further references see pages *93*, *94*.

were undoubtedly much higher.

During the night, the British slipped away and a few days later reached New York, where they were put under blockade when the Continental Army reached White Plains on June 30. Lee demanded a court martial to review his actions at Monmouth Court House, and was somewhat harshly judged guilty of disobedience to orders, poor conduct of the retreat, and disrespect of Washington. As a result Lee resigned.

France Enters the War

War between France and Great Britain broke out on June 17, but in far-sighted anticipation, the French had sent Admiral Jean Baptiste le Comte d'Estaing from France in May with a force of 11 ships of the line and transports carrying 4,000 men. Admiral Howe lacked British naval strength to challenge this French fleet. Thus, the strategic initiative thus passed to the Americans and their French allies during the late summer of 1778. Washington was determined to take full advantage of all that this offered.

The French fleet arrived in American waters on July 8 off Sandy Hook and immediately implemented a naval blockade of New York to match that of Washington on land. The American and French commanders then decided on a combined land and sea assault on New York until d'Estaing called off the French naval attack. The admiral feared that his deeply laden ships would be stranded on the bar running between Staten Island and Sandy Hook. The allied commanders switched their attentions to the weaker British toehold in the area at Newport.

Lying as it does on an island with difficult approaches, Newport presented considerable problems for d'Estaing and Sullivan, the local commander with whom d'Estaing worked after arriving in Narragansett Bay. The plan finally adopted had serious flaws: the French ships were to force the passage on the western side of the island, and the Americans were to cross over and attack the British from the east. The French arrived off Newport on July 29 and forced their passage. Sullivan's forces began to cross to the island on August 8, and d'Estaing began to disembark the French troops. Unfortunately for the allies, Admiral Howe arrived from New York with a reinforced fleet, forcing d'Estaing to re-embark his soldiers and put out to sea to engage Howe. As the two naval forces maneuvered for position off Newport, both fleets were dispersed by a great storm on August 12. Howe's ships fell back to New York to refit, and those of d'Estaing went to Boston for the same purpose. Sullivan was left with no option but to call off the attack on Newport and try to extricate his forces from their untenable position as best he could.

An Early Failure for Franco-American Cooperation

This first effort at allied cooperation therefore ended as a total fiasco. Then, d'Estaing decided that matters in the West Indies were more important to French interests. On November 4 the French weighed anchor and sailed for the West Indies. This failure of cooperation dashed all Washington's hopes for a decisive American victory in 1778. In 1779, the French were forced by British activities to focus their attention on the West Indies, so the British were able to regain the initiative on the American mainland. The following years saw the Revolutionary War increasingly caught up in complex European affairs. In June 1779 Spain declared war on Great Britain. In December 1780 the Netherlands also became involved following a British declaration of war in exasperation about Dutch trade with the United States. Neither of these European powers actually allied themselves with the fledgling United States. Nevertheless, Great Britain had to guard against the possibility of an invasion of England, and she undertook operations on a global scale against her three adversaries. Smaller forces were therefore available for American operations.

Yet the Americans were not able to take any real advantage of this British weakening, for their own war effort was made increasingly difficult by war weariness, insufficient finance, poor central administration and the absence of any strong direction of the war effort. The British were determined to hold onto their American possessions. Although they were unable to match the numbers of men available in earlier campaigns, they were generally able to field in America an army larger than that which Washington could muster.

Development of American Sea Power

During this period, there was a marked increase in American seafaring activity. Lacking a navy with which to challenge the British in a conventional naval war, the Continental Congress had already authorized the construction of 13 frigates. It also issued letters of marque that allowed up to 2,000 merchant ships to be fitted as privateers manned by up to 70,000 men. The privateers never reached this number, peaking at 449 ships during 1781, but their efforts were a serious worry to the British, especially with their raids in the sea lanes connecting Great Britain with the West Indies. In 1778, the first of America's great naval heroes emerged in John Paul Jones, who had been born in Scotland and learned his

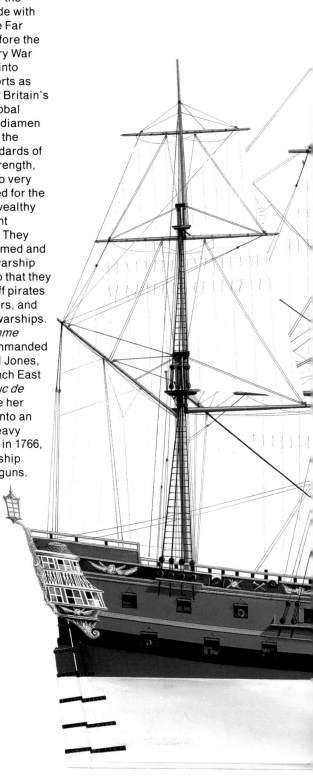

These fine ships were built by the Honourable East India Company for the valuable trade with India and the Far East, and before the Revolutionary War often sailed into American ports as part of Great Britain's pattern of global trade. The Indiamen were built to the highest standards of structural strength, but were also very well equipped for the carriage of wealthy and important passengers. They were also armed and manned to warship standards so that they could fight off pirates and privateers, and even small warships. The *Bonhomme Richard*, commanded by John Paul Jones, was the French East Indiaman *Duc de Duras* before her conversion into an American heavy frigate. Built in 1766, this 900-ton ship mounted 40 guns.

COMBAT MEMORABLE

seafaring as a slave trader and smuggler. In his first cruise, between April and May 1778, Jones took his Ranger from the French port of Brest into British waters. After terrorizing shipping in the Irish Sea, he landed at Whitehaven on the northwest coast of England to spike the guns of the local fort. He then crossed to St. Mary's Island in the Scilly Isles to capture the home of the Earl of Selkirk. Jones then cruised off northern Ireland, captured H.M.S. *Drake* off Carrickfergus and took her into Brest.

Triumph of the *Bonhomme Richard*

During his second cruise, in the *Bonhomme Richard* converted from a French East Indiaman, Jones sailed again into British waters. On September 23, 1779 off Flamborough Head he attacked a British convoy sailing on the Baltic route and was heavily engaged by the escorting frigate, H.M.S. *Serapis*. The two ships fought one of the most remarkable single-ship actions of all time. The *Serapis* set the *Bonhomme Richard* on fire before the British captain called on Jones to surrender. Responding "I have not yet begun to fight!," Jones breathed new hope into his men. They boarded the British frigate after shooting away her mainmast and finally forced a

British surrender after the *Serapis* gun deck had been swept by an explosion touched off by an American grenade. Jones transferred his crew from the sinking *Bonhomme Richard* and sailed the *Serapis* into Brest.

While these events were on the horizon, Washington was consolidating his blockade of New York. Monmouth Court House was the last general battle fought in the northern theater. Washington was determined to prevent any further British eruption from New York. The American

Above left: Brigadier General Anthony Wayne agreed with de Lafayette that a more cautious plan should have been adopted in the approach to the British before the Battle of Monmouth Court House. Such a strategy would have resulted in an attack on the British rear instead of the general engagement that took place.

PEARSON ET PAUL IONES

Wayne with a force of the new light infantry against the British garrison of Stony Point. Delivered with the bayonet after a stealthy approach, the American recapture of Stony Point on the night of July 15-16 achieved the useful military result of removing the British threat to West Point. It was more significant as an indication that the Americans were well on the way to mastering the skills of light infantry and bayonet fighting. Wayne was unsuccessful in his attempt to recapture Verplanck's Point, and the British soon retook Stony Point.

Static Warfare in New York

The war around New York had now taken on the character of a strictly limited war involving skirmishes and raids designed to test each side's watchfulness. A typical raid took place on August 18, when a small force under Major Henry "Light-horse Harry" Lee recaptured Paulus Hook on the New Jersey side of New York harbor.

The Battle of Saratoga had removed any real threat of a British invasion of New York from Canada. The British sought to exploit their good relations with the Indian tribes in order to stir up trouble for

Above: The single-ship action between the *Bonhomme Richard* and *Serapis* remains a classic of its type.
Above right: John Paul Jones was the first U.S. naval hero. In his first commission, he captured eight British ships and destroyed another eight.

defensive line was centered on West Point, on the western bank of the Hudson River. Clinton made no concerted effort to breach or even attack it. Instead, Clinton hoped to tempt the Americans forward of their line with major raids on May 31, 1779 against the unfinished forts at Verplanck's Point and Stony Point. Washington was too clever to take the British bait. Seeing that Washington had avoided the trap, Clinton pulled back his main body to New York. Then Washington responded by launching Major General

Left: The storming of Stony Point on July 15-16, 1779, by Major General Anthony Wayne's light infantry.

Below: American success in the Battle of Stony Point removed the British threat to West Point and confirmed the fighting abilities of the newly created light infantry arm.

Henry Lee played a modest but useful part in the Revolutionary War. He is best remembered as the major general who in 1794 commanded the militia force sent to western Pennsylvania to deal with the "Whiskey Rebellion."

the Americans all along the frontier, and to tie down American forces in duties far from the main centers of the war. Wherever possible, the activities of the pro-British Iroquois were aided by loyalist groups, and considerable disturbance was achieved in the frontier regions.

However, Clinton's relative inactivity in New York gave Washington the chance to deal with the Indian attacks. The main bases for these loyalist-led raids were Fort Niagara and Detroit. From here, the Indians swept through the Mohawk valley of New York (notably on November 11, 1778), the Wyoming valley of Pennysylvania (notably on July 3, 1778), and the

new American settlements in Kentucky. Other massacres were perpetrated by the Johnson family, a notoriously bloodthirsty group, and by John and Walter Butler. In August 1778, Washington launched a punitive expedition into Pennsylvania and northwest New York under the command of Sullivan with Lee as his deputy. The expedition laid waste the villages of the Iroquois and finally trimmed this British operation to manageable size by defeating the Indians plus a number of loyalists in the Battle of Newtown on August 29. The expedition then returned in September 1778 after mopping up some last pockets of resistance.

American Successes in Virginia

Similar in its effect was the expedition launched by the state of Virginia in the winter of 1778-79. A force of 175 militiamen, supposedly raised for the defense of Kentucky, was led by Lieutenant Colonel George Rogers Clark. He conducted a small campaign of great tactical skill that overran all the British outposts in the areas of what are today Illinois and Indiana, culminating in the capture of Vincennes on February 25, 1779. Neither Sullivan nor Clark had been able to tackle the main British positions at Fort Niagara and Detroit, but the effect of the two expeditions was to limit the scope of the Indian raids. Clark's capture of Vincennes also allowed the United States, during negotiations for the Treaty of Paris in 1783, to put in a successful claim for the region between the Allegheny Mountains and the Mississippi River, an area much greater than that of the original 13 states.

As the revised nature of the war began to become clear to the British, late in 1778 they decided to switch the focus of the main effort farther to the south. Here loyalists had kept the southern colonies in a state of ferment for two years. Small-scale operations between loyalists and American patriots had been frequent, but no major operations had been attempted by either side. In the Carolinas and Georgia, loyalist strength was higher than in the middle and northern colonies. The British felt that loyalist operations would be easier to support, as the regions were relatively close to the British bases in the West Indies, where major naval forces were stationed to guard against French ambitions. The British plan was to return the three southern states to British rule one by one and use the area as the major base from which to attack northward and reconquer the other 10 colonies.

The British Invasion of Georgia

Moving forward from the British colony of East Florida, a small British force under Major General Augustine Prevost began to overrun Georgia in the winter of 1778-79. This southernmost of the rebellious states had become a British colony only in 1733 and was still very sparsely populated. On November 8, 1778 Lieutenant Colonel Archibald Campbell was moved by sea from New York with 3,500 men of Clinton's army. On December 29, he captured Savannah at the mouth of the Savannah River, crushing the defense of 1,000 American militiamen commanded by Brigadier General Robert Howe. In January 1779 Prevost arrived in Savannah after his advance through Georgia, and Campbell advanced up the Savannah to take Augusta on January 29. An American force under Ashe was sent from Charleston, South Carolina, in February to handle Campbell's detachment. But south of Augusta, in the Battle of Briar Creek, the British decisively beat back the Americans on March 3.

Alarmed by the obvious implications of this revised British strategy, the Continental Congress sent Major General Benjamin Lincoln to Charleston in December 1778 as commander of the Southern Army, which also received reinforcements

The expedition of Lieutenant Colonel George Rogers Clark crosses the Wabash River while approaching Vincennes, which was captured for the United States on February 25, 1779.

Savannah
For further references see pages
91, 94, 95, *96*, 112, 130.

The Naval flag flown by the U.S. Navy ship *Alliance* in European waters, October, 1799.

In the campaign in the south, the British hoped to exploit the availability of many loyalists to bolster their own strength while pitting the American

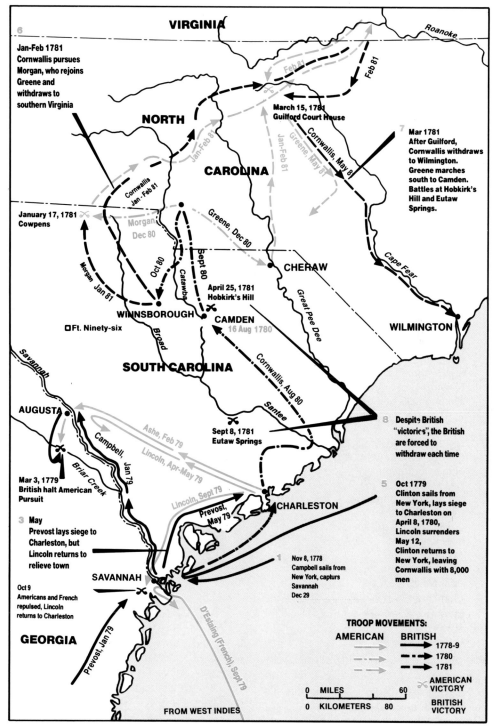

Jan-Feb 1781 Cornwallis pursues Morgan, who rejoins Greene and withdraws to southern Virginia

March 15, 1781 Guilford Court House

7 **Mar 1781** After Guilford, Cornwallis withdraws to Wilmington. Greene marches south to Camden. Battles at Hobkirk's Hill and Eutaw Springs.

January 17, 1781 Cowpens

April 25, 1781 Hobkirk's Hill

□ Ft. Ninety-six

CAMDEN 16 Aug 1780

WINNSBOROUGH

WILMINGTON

CHERAW

Sept 8, 1781 Eutaw Springs

8 Despite British "victories", the British are forced to withdraw each time

AUGUSTA

Mar 3, 1779 British halt American Pursuit

3 **May** Prevost lays siege to Charleston, but Lincoln returns to relieve town

5 Oct 1779 Clinton sails from New York, lays siege to Charleston on April 8, 1780, Lincoln surrenders May 12, Clinton returns to New York, leaving Cornwallis with 8,000 men

Oct 9 Americans and French repulsed, Lincoln returns to Charleston

SAVANNAH

CHARLESTON

Nov 8, 1778 Campbell sails from New York, captures Savannah Dec 29

GEORGIA

FROM WEST INDIES

TROOP MOVEMENTS:

AMERICAN	BRITISH
	1778-9
	1780
	1781

✂ AMERICAN VICTORY

BRITISH VICTORY

| 0 | MILES | 60 |
| 0 | KILOMETERS | 80 |

from the Continental Army. Lincoln's orders were to build up American strength and then to strike against the British in Georgia and, by logical extension, South Carolina,. In April, Lincoln decided on another overland advance from Charleston for the recapture of Augusta. As he was approaching the town he received news of British moves on the coast and headed back to Charleston. On the coast an effort was made by Prevost to take Port Royal, halfway between Savannah and Charlston, but it had been repulsed February 3 by American forces commanded by William Moultrie. Prevost moved against Charleston again in May,

Private, Continental Marines (1779)

Although marines are known to have been in existence since May 1775, when they are mentioned in the payroll of the *Enterprise*, the official birthday of the US Marine Corps is November 10, 1775, when the Continental Congress ordered the raising of two marine battalions. The first recruiting center for the Continental Marines was in Philadelphia at the Tun Tavern, whose landlord was commissioned into the Marine Committee of the Continental Congress. A marine uniform was approved by Congress that consisted of a green coat with white facings, and for officers a silver epaulet on the right shoulder. In 1779, the color of the facings was changed to red, probably because of the shortage of white material in Philadelphia, which was the depot for the Continental Marines. The Continental Marines were disbanded at the end of the Revolutionary War and then raised once more in July 1798 as the Marine Corps.

but he was forced to pull back once more by the arrival of Lincoln's force from Augusta. Prevost fought off an attack by Lincoln at Stone Ferry on June 19 and returned safely to Savannah.

Warfare between Patriots and American "Tories"

While these more formal military operations were proceeding, the small-scale warfare between loyalists and American patriots continued. On February 14, a loyalist brigade was defeated by Colonel Andrew Pickens's militia at Kettle Creek. North Carolina and Virginia militia units raided the villages of the troublesome Chickamauga Indians in Tennessee. In May Admiral Sir George Collier's British squadron burned Portsmouth and other towns on the coast of Virginia.

Meanwhile d'Estaing's French squadron had been operating in the West Indies. On July 6, 1779, the French met Admiral John Byron's British force in the

Above: The largest single American reverse in the Revolutionary War was the loss of Charleston, which was surrendered by Major General Benjamin Lincoln on May 12, 1780.

Right: French support for the American cause was linked directly to their opposition to the British in control of the western hemisphere. In July 1779, the French under Admiral d'Estaing took Grenada. This scene depicts French officers cutting off their epaulets to decorate the shoulders of grenadiers who had fought with distinction.

93

Battle of Grenada. Although the French fared better in the inconclusive engagement, d'Estaing decided to return to American waters. On September 3, the French ships appeared off Savannah and captured two British warships as well as two transports. The French fleet then landed 6,000 troops to take Savannah under siege on September 12. Lincoln moved south with 1,350 Americans to take part in the siege, giving the allies a total strength of 7,350 men against the 3,500 under Prevost's command. But the defenses of Savannah were formidable, and the allies made very limited progress. D'Estaing was worried that his fleet, unable to use Savannah harbor, might fall prey to seasonal storms and ordered a general assault in an effort to speed progress. The French warships attempted a bombardment of the British positions with no success. On October 8, the allies advanced for the general assault in five columns. The British had been warned of the planned attack by a deserter and were fully prepared. Fighting from behind their prepared defenses, the British were able to push back each allied attack in the hardest fighting of the war since the Battle of Bunker Hill. The British suffered 150 casualties, but the allies lost more than 800 men, including the invaluable Pulaski. D'Estaing broke off the siege, re-embarked his men and sailed once more for the West Indies. This second attempt at allied cooperation had failed as dismally as the first at Newport, and the result was a serious American loss of faith in the French. The British and loyalists, on the other hand, were delighted with their victory, which seemed to offer great hope for continued success in the south.

Clinton Moves to Savannah

In New York, Clinton had come under increasing pressure from the British government to push the southern campaign as hard as possible. The departure of d'Estaing for the West Indies had restored command of the sea to the British. This offered the possibility for operations that would benefit from greater strategic mobility than Washington

could hope to achieve. On October 11, the British garrison of Newport was evacuated. Soon, Clinton began to pull back his New York outposts and, leaving von Knyphausen in command of a New York garrison much reduced in responsibilities and numbers, sailed with 8,000 men for Savannah. The British left New York on December 26 and, after a stopover on the Virginia coast, arrived off South Carolina. With the arrival of Clinton and his army, the British could now put into the field some 14,000 men, a number far superior to that of Lincoln, who could be reinforced only slowly and in smaller numbers by the difficult overland routes available to Washington.

The British attack on Charleston was planned with great care as a combined operation involving the army and the navy. It began on February 11, 1780, when British troops cautiously surrounded the city. Clinton landed his forces on John's Island south of the city and moved up the west bank of the Ashley River until he was at a point north of Charleston on its promontory between the Ashley and Cooper Rivers. At the insistence of the South Carolina authorities, Lincoln had prepared his defenses across the promontory just north of the city. On March 29, Clinton's force crossed the Ashley and deployed across the promontory, cutting off the city and its defenders. The British action was completed on April 8, when British warships brushed aside the limited defense of Fort Moultrie south of the city and sealed the city off from the sea.

The Americans Lose Charleston

Clinton decided that tried and true measures were best. The British used the traditional system of advancing trench lines in siege of Charleston, which was also bombarded by the ships of Admiral Marriot Arbuthnot's squadron. On May 12, Lincoln bowed to the inevitable and surrendered his command. A total of 5,466 fighting men were captured, together with large quantities of artillery, small arms, and ammunition, to make the fall of Charleston the single greatest American disaster of the war.

Men of Lieutenant Colonel Francis Marion's guerrilla outfit cross the Pee Dee River during their campaign against loyalists in 1778.

His task complete, Clinton sailed for New York again, leaving Cornwallis and a force of 8,000 men in the south to "pacify" South Carolina. Cornwallis went about his task with a ruthless determination. The free hand given to the cavalry regiment commanded by the loyalist Lieutenant Colonel Sir Banastre Tarleton resulted in levels of brutality that turned most American opinion decisively against the British. The worst of Tarleton's excesses took place in the Battle of Waxhaw Creek on May 29, when a regiment of 350 Virginians under Colonel Abraham Buford was trapped just after crossing from North into South Carolina. Buford tried to surrender, but Tarleton's men massacred most of the Americans. News of such massacres inflamed American feeling still more against the British. This led to a further increase in guerrilla operations against the British occupation by bands under the command of men such as Lieutenant Colonel Francis Marion (the

"Swamp Fox"), Brigadier General Thomas Sumter, and Brigadier General Andrew Pickens.

From his main bases at Beaufort, Charleston, Georgetown, and Savannah, Cornwallis and his regulars, supported by a large numbers of loyalists, tried to hold down an area that stretched as far west as Fort Ninety-Six. It was an impossible task. In effect, a civil war raged through South Carolina, with the British completely unable to pick the fruit of their purely military victory at Charleston in the face of steadily increasing grass-roots opposition. To this extent, the Charleston campaign echoed the Saratoga campaign of three years earlier.

Washington sent south additional American forces. On June 22, Major General de Kalb arrived in Hillsboro, North Carolina, with the 900 men of two very understrength brigades as the core of a new Southern Army. The American commander-in-chief knew that by itself

Top: The British used traditional methods of advancing trench lines in the siege of Charleston, which was also bombarded by the ships of Admiral Arbuthnot's squadron.

Center: The death of Brigadier General Johann de Kalb in the Battle of Camden on August 16, 1780.

Bottom: On October 9, 1779, the Americans and French launched a combined attack on the British base at Savannah, but were driven back after severe fighting.

Sergeant, New York Regiment (1779)

French influence is evident in this uniform of a sergeant in comparatively light combat order rather than heavier marching order. Apart from his musket, the most interesting features are the crossbelts supporting ammunition pouches that are tucked far enough toward the back to leave the man's front clear for easy movement of the weapon, and the leather harness supporting the man's pack of field equipment, probably a blanket, clothes, and food. The musket is a typical flintlock of the period, either a French Charleville model of 1763 or an American copy of it. Comparatively large numbers of these weapons were supplied by France, and variations on the basic model were reproduced by more than 200 gunsmiths in Maryland, Massachusetts, Pennsylvania, and Rhode Island in calibers ranging from 0·72 to 0·80 inch.

LUCAS 89

this force could achieve virtually nothing, but hoped that, around this nucleus of regular forces, a growing number of militia units would gather. But without consulting Washington, the Continental Congress in July appointed the hero of Saratoga, Gates as commander of the new Southern Army. That this was a poor choice was soon demonstrated. Rather than control and amplify the already successful guerrilla war in South Carolina while he concentrated and trained his forces, Gates opted for an advance with a force of 4,000 men, mainly militiamen, into South Carolina, where he planned to capture the British outpost at Camden.

The Battle of Camden

Cornwallis moved out from Charleston with some 2,200 British regulars and, after crossing the lower reaches of the Santee River hastened northwest to meet Gates outside Camden on August 15. During the early morning of August 16, Gates deployed his militiamen on the left and his Continentals, under de Kalb, on the right. The militia were still moving into position as Cornwallis attacked, and almost immediately broke and fled in total disarray. This left de Kalb's men hopelessly exposed on their left flank. The Battle of Camden was a British victory. The British infantry destroyed de Kalb's command, while Tarleton's cavalry pursued the routed Americans for 30 miles. Gates managed to escape, moving so fast that he covered the 160 miles to Hillsboro in only three days. The American survivors of the battle slowly straggled back to Hillsboro, but only 800 men rejoined the commander. Nine hundred men, including de Kalb, had been killed, and another 1,000 captured. This disastrous American episode was made worse by the fact that Tarleton caught and virtually destroyed Sumter's guerrilla force, sent by Gates to

For his part in the treason of Benedict Arnold, Major John Andre was sentenced to death. The calmness with which he received the sentence impressed all those present. Arnold escaped, receiving 6,315 pounds sterling and a commission in the rank of brigadier general from the British.

raid a British wagon train, at Fishing Creek on August 18. South Carolina remained in British hands.

American Fortunes at Their Lowest Ebb

August 1780 can perhaps be regarded as the lowest ebb in American fortunes during the Revolutionary War. Matters could only get better. The Continental Congress returned the southern command to Washington, who appointed his "right arm," Greene, to command the Southern Army in place of Gates. This was one of the last appointments in a series of shuffles that went a long way toward removing many of the difficulties under which the Continental Army had been laboring. Supply failings and the decreasing value of Continental currency had hit the Continental Army hard. There had even been a mutiny by the troops at

Morristown on May 23, 1780, after a winter in which the army had suffered even worse hardships than at Valley Forge. The mutiny had been quelled without delay, but the problem was still there. The Continental Congress tried to pass the problem to the individual states by demanding that each state provide the clothing for its own contingent and provide a quota of other supplies for the complete army. The system could not and did not work. The states were slow in meeting their quotas, and when supplies were provided, it was almost never at the right time or place. Greene had resigned as quartermaster general early in 1780, and the difficulties of maintaining the Continental Army became impossible as men refused to come forward when they knew that they would receive neither pay nor essential supplies. A militia statistic reveals the severity of the situation: in 1780, less than half the number of men were enlisted for one year's service than

The powder tester was an essential item of kit for proving the effectiveness of the gunpowder in each barrel. Based on a pistol, the tester was loaded with a standard charge and fired. The gases generated by the powder as it was fired then drove the heavy curved lever from the muzzle, and so turned the curved indicator scale. From this the firer could read a powder figure for comparison with those provided by other firings. Because of manufacturing defects and fraud, British powder at the time of the Revolutionary War was much inferior to that made by the French. This resulted in an inquiry which revised the system effectively. British powder was the best in the world by the time of the French Revolutionary and Napoleonic Wars that started only 15 years after the end of the Revolutionary War.

Gunner, Continental Artillery (1780)

Knox's Brigade of Artillery served with the main body of the Continental Army between 1777 and 1783. The brigade was made up of four battalions each of 12 companies, a company from the Regiment of Artillery Artificers, and the civilian drivers. The task of the artificers was maintenance of the brigade's technical equipment. The uniform shown here was adopted in 1779 with a dark blue coat with red facings and yellow lacing. Artillerymen carried full infantry equipment (including a musket for personal defense) and this man is also notable for his striped overall trousers and a drag rope. Non-commissioned officers were distinguished by their two epaulets, those for corporals in yellow worsted and those for sergeants in yellow silk.

De Rochambeau had serious reservations about the willingness of the Americans to sustain a major war effort.

and could not seriously plan any offensive with the Americans. De Rochambeau had already warned his government: "Send us troops, ships and money, but do not count on these people or their resources, they have neither money nor credit, their forces exist only momentarily..." Another French commander thought that the British needed to persuade only one highly placed American to turn traitor to secure an easy and victorious end to the war.

The Treason of Benedict Arnold

In fact, Clinton had already found such a traitor in Benedict Arnold, who was offered large sums of money by the British. Feeling that he had been slighted by the Continental Congress and that the Americans were now in effect fighting for France, Arnold accepted the British offer. He managed to secure for himself command of West Point and then schemed to deliver the position to the British. With the capture of a British agent, Major John Andre, on September 21, Washington learned of the traitorous plan and foiled it. Arnold escaped, received a large sum of money from the British, and was commissioned as a brigadier general in the British service. Andre was hanged as a spy.

had volunteered in 1776 for three years' service. The May 1780 mutiny at Morristown was an obvious result of the problem. The failure to solve the problem is indicated by further mutinies at Morristown (January 1, 1781 and May 1781) and Pompton (May 1781), all put down with some severity.

The Americans' problems were a source of great satisfaction to the British, who once again came to the conclusion that they would now win the war without undue difficulty. But the Americans' problems were also a major worry for the French. From July 11, 1780 a French army of 4,000 men under General Jean Baptiste de Vimeur le Comte de Rochambeau had been landed at the Newport base evacuated by the British. It was planned that this army, along with its supporting force of seven ships of line under Admiral de Termay, would then cooperate with American forces for an offensive against Clinton's New York army. But the French had been blockaded by British warships

Despite all these problems, which reached their lowest point with Arnold's treason, the Americans somehow managed to build the foundations for a continued effort in 1781. Finances were put on a sounder footing by Robert Morris, a wealthy Philadelphian who was persuaded by the Continental Congress to become Superintendent of Finance The Continental Army's supply problems were eased by the appointment of Colonel Timothy Pickering to replace Greene, putting an able administrator at the head of the army's supply system. The Board of War was abolished, and a new Secretary of War was found in Lee, who had been exchanged after the Charleston disaster. Lee personally handled with greater speed and skill many of the tasks that had previously been undertaken by committees of the Board of War. Lee also

I Benedict Arnold Major General
do acknowledge the UNITED STATES of AME-
RICA to be Free, Independent and Sovereign States, and
declare that the people thereof owe no allegiance or obedience to George the Third, King of Great-Britain; and I
renounce, refuse and abjure any allegiance or obedience to
him; and I do Swear that I will, to the ut-
moft of my power, fupport, maintain and defend the faid
United States againft the faid King George the Third, his
heirs and fucceffors, and his or their abettors, affiftants and
adherents, and will ferve the faid United States in the office of
Major General which I now hold, with
fidelity, according to the beft of my fkill and underftanding.

Sworn before me this 30th. May 1778 at the Artillery Park Valley Forge B Arnold H Knox

The oath of allegiance signed by Major General Benedict Arnold at Valley Forge was witnessed on May 30, 1778, by Henry Knox.

worked closely with Pickering to improve the Continental Army's supply situation. Particularly important was Lee's abandonment of devalued paper money and the setting up of a temporary practice of private contracts, backed by his own credit as guarantee that the contractors would eventually be paid in gold.

The Militia Begins to Come of Age

The first concrete evidence that the Americans were recovering from the disasters at Charleston and Camden was provided by the militia, whom the British had come to hold in low esteem. De Rochambeau had even reported: "...when they are about to be attacked in their own homes they assemble...to defend themselves." Clinton had reluctantly agreed by this time to the plan suggested by Cornwallis for an invasion of North Carolina. As a first move, Cornwallis sent Major Patrick Ferguson, who had been very successful in raising loyalist forces in the back country of South

Carolina, into North Carolina. Ferguson was to raise loyalist forces that would then meet Cornwallis's main advance at Charlotte, which had begun in September from Camden. News of Ferguson's advance with his 1,100 "American Volunteers" spread immediate alarm among the "over-mountain men" of western North Carolina, southwestern Virginia, and what is now eastern Tennessee.

The Battle of King's Mountain

These three areas combined to create an elite force of 1,400 mounted riflemen. They gathered at the Catawba River in western North Carolina under the command of Colonels Isaac Shelby and Richard Campbell, and then moved forward to tackle Ferguson. The two forces, among whom the only non-American was Ferguson, met at King's Mountain close to the border of North and South Carolina on October 7, 1780. The result was a decisive defeat for the loyalists: Ferguson and many of his men were killed, some while trying to surrender,

Major General Lord Cornwallis was the British commander in the southern campaign, The lack of effective cooperation between Cornwallis and Sir Henry Clinton in New York was a major factor in the eventual British defeat.

and most of the survivors were captured.

King's Mountain had the same effect on Cornwallis's plan as Bennington had exercised on Burgoyne's scheme. The North Carolina loyalists were now unwilling to support Cornwallis, who was then forced to begin a rain-sodden withdrawal toward Winnsborough, South Carolina during October. The British retreat was harassed constantly by American militia. So dismal was the prospect for Cornwallis that Clinton was forced to reinforce Cornwallis with 2,500 men who would otherwise have been used to establish a base in Virginia. Having achieved their immediate task, the militiamen then followed their normal, unfortunate practice and returned home. Arriving to assume command of the Southern Army on December 2, Greene found that Charlotte had only 1,482 men, of whom 949 were at Charlottetals, all poorly clothed and equipped. By the middle of the month reinforcements from Washington had reached Greene, bolstering American strength to 3,000 men including 1,400 Continentals. Clinton's reinforcements had meanwhile reached Cornwallis, who had an overall strength of 4,000 better clothed and equipped regulars.

The experienced Greene knew full well the dangers involved in dividing his command in the face of a numerically superior enemy, but also knew that he had no alternative but to do so. His army could not grow in strength on the meager supplies available in Charlotte, but divided into two parts, it could live off the land and grow in capability and mobility. A divided Southern Army could also provide two cores around which militia forces could gather. The American movement began on December 20. Greene himself took half of the army southeast to Cheraw Hill on the Great Pee Dee River in South Carolina. Brigadier General Daniel Morgan took the other half west across the upper reaches of the Catawba River, also in South Carolina. The two parts of the Southern Army were separated by 140 miles, a distance that according to the conventional military wisdom of the day spelled disaster for the Americans.

Continued British Pressure in North Carolina

Cornwallis was still determined to invade and capture North Carolina for the British cause. Ignoring the sensible warnings of Clinton, he virtually stripped the main British base at Charleston by bringing up additional men and nearly all the available supplies. Faced with Greene's divided army, Cornwallis decided to do much the same thing, though in this instance the British force was divided into three parts. One part was sent southeast under Brigadier General Alexander Leslie to Camden with the task of checking Greene at Cheraw Hill. The second part, with 1,100 fast-moving infantry and cavalry under Tarleton was launched northwest to trap Morgan's detachment, The third, under Cornwallis himself paralleled Tarleton slightly farther to the east with the object of intercepting any of Morgan's detachment that escaped from Tarleton.

The British movements started in January 1781, and on January 17, Tarleton caught up with Morgan at a spot west of King's Mountain known as the Cowpens, an open area with scattering of timber about six miles from the Broad River. This ground was not of the Americans' choice, for Morgan had been trying to get his force across the river. But Morgan managed a tactical masterstroke that made best use of his mixed force, only one-quarter of

them Continentals. Morgan deployed these regulars on a hill in the center of his position, leaving the flanks completely open. In front of this main position, he located two lines of militia riflemen with instructions that the first line was to fire only two volleys before falling back on the second line. The combined lines were then to fire until pressed by the British and then fall back behind the Continentals and so create a reserve. Behind the hill Morgan placed Lieutenant Colonel William Washington's cavalry with orders to charge the British at the decisive moment. Morgan's tactical plan was excellent, and he made sure that every man knew exactly what he was to do.

The Battle of Cowpens

Immediately after he encountered Morgan, Tarleton ordered the attack. His force moved up in regular order against the forward-deployed militia. They inflicted

The arms of the United States reflect the nation's varied and sometimes bloody origins.

Lieutenant Colonel William Washington, the American cavalry commander, fights with Lieutenant Colonel Sir Banastre Tarleton in the Battle of Cowpens (sometimes known as the Battle of the Cowpens) on January 17, 1781. The battle was small in scope, but was a decisive tactical victory for the Americans and a classic example of the double envelopment.

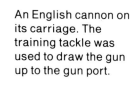

An English cannon on
its carriage. The
training tackle was
used to draw the gun
up to the gun port.

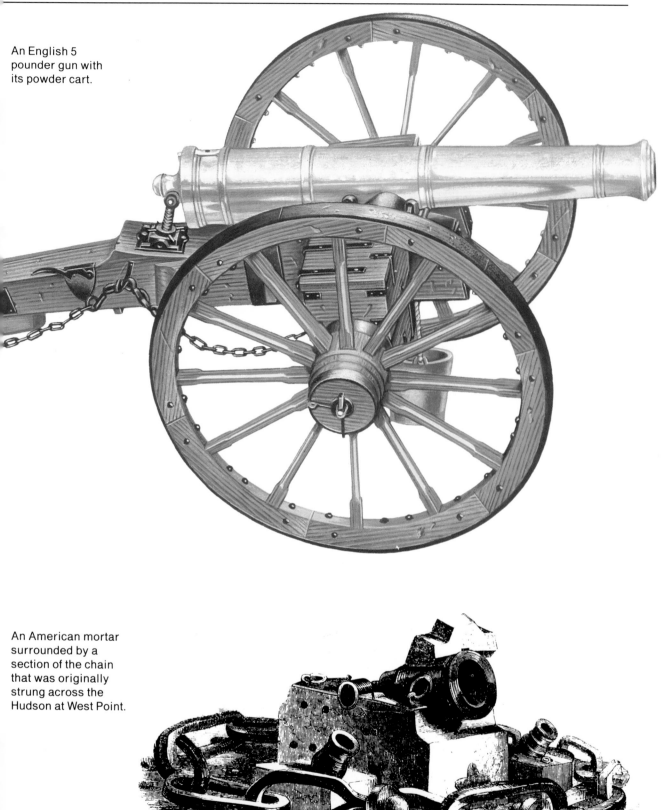

An English 5 pounder gun with its powder cart.

An American mortar surrounded by a section of the chain that was originally strung across the Hudson at West Point.

107

The Revolution in the South featured bitter civil war between whigs and tories. Sixteen year old Thomas Young fought in many guerrilla actions and served at the important battles of King's Mountain (October 7, 1780) and Cowpens (January 17, 1781).

''I was born in Laurens District, South-Carolina, on the 17th June 1764. My father, Thomas Young, soon after removed to Union District, where I have lived to this day. In the spring of 1780, I think in April, Colonel Brandon was encamped with a party of seventy or eighty whigs, about five miles from Union Court House, where Christopher Young now lives. Their object was to collect forces for the approaching campaign, and to keep a check upon the tories. They had taken prisoner, one Adam Steedham, as vile a tory as ever lived. By some means, Steedham escaped during the night, and notified the tories of Brandon's position. The whigs were attached by a large body of the enemy before day, and completely routed. On that occasion, my brother, John Young, was murdered. I shall never forget my feelings, when told of his death. I do not believe I had ever used an oath before that day, but then I tore open my bosom, and swore that I would never rest until I had avenged his death. Subsequently, many tories felt the weight of my arm, and around Steedham's neck I fastened the rope, as a reward for his cruelties. On the next day, I left home in my shirt sleeves, and joined Brandon's Party. Chr. Brandon and I joined at the same time, and the first engagement we were in was at Stallions', in York District.

We had been told of a party of tories, then stationed at Stallions'; a detachment of about fifty whigs, under Colonel Brandon, moved to attack them. Before we arrived at the house in which they were fortified, we were divided into two parties; Captain Love, with a party of sixteen, of whom I was one, marched to attach the front, while Colonel Brandon, with the remainder, made a circuit to intercept those who should attempt to escape and also to attack the rear. Mrs. Stallions was a sister of Captain Love, and, on the approach of her brother, she ran out and begged him not to fire upon the house. She ran back to the house, and sprang upon the door step, which was pretty high. At this moment, the house was attacked, in the rear, by Colonel Brandon's party, and Mrs. Stallions was killed by a ball shot at random through the opposite door. At the same moment with Brandon's attack, our party raised a shout and rushed forward. We fired several rounds, which were briskly returned. It was not long, however, before the tories ran up a flag, first upon the end of a gun; but, as that did not look exactly peaceful, a ball was put through the fellow's arm, and, in a few minutes, the flag was raised on a ramrod, when we ceased firing. While we were fighting, a man was seen running through an open field, near us. I raised my gun to shoot him, when some of our party exclaimed, ''don't shoot, he is one of our own men.'' I drew down my gun, and in a moment he halted, wheeled round, and fired at us. Old Squire Kennedy, who was an excellent marksman, raised his rifle and brought him down. We had but one wounded, William Kennedy, who was shot by my side, through the wrist and thigh. The loss of the tories was two killed, four wounded, and twenty-eight prisoners, whom we sent to Charlotte, North-Carolina. After the fight, Love and Stallions met and shed bitter tears. Stallions was dismissed, on parole, to bury his wife and arrange his affairs.

The next engagement I was in, was at King's Mountain, South-Carolina, on the 17th October, 1780. When our division came up to the northern base of the mountain, we dismounted, and Colonel Roebuck drew us a little to the left, and commenced the attack. Ben Hollingsworth and myself took right up the side of the mountain, and fought, from tree to tree, our way to the summit. I recollect I stood behind one tree and fired, until the bark was nearly all knocked off, and my eyes pretty well filled with it. One fellow shaved me pretty close, for his bullet took a piece out of my gun-stock. Before I was aware of it, I found myself apparently between my own regiment and the enemy, as I judged, from seeing the paper which the whigs wore in their hats, and the pine knots the tories wore in theirs, these being the badges of distinction. On the top of the mountain, in the thickest of the fight, I saw Colonel Williams fall, and a braver and a better man never died upon a battle-field. I ran to his assistance, for I loved him as a father; he had ever been so kind to me, and almost always carried a cake in his pocket for me and his little son, Joseph. They carried him into a tent, and sprinkled some water into his face. He revived, and his first words were, "For God's sake, boys, don't give up the hill!" He died the next day, and was buried not far from the field of his glory. Daniel and Joseph Williams, his sons, were both massacred by the tories at Hays' Station, where Daniel first threw his father's pistols into the burning house, rather than they should go into the hands of the tories.

We arrived at the field of Cowpens about sunset, and were then told that there we should meet the enemy. It was upon this occasion I was more perfectly convinced of General Morgan's qualifications to command militia,

than I had ever before been. He went among the volunteers, helped them to fix their swords, joked with them about their sweethearts, told them to keep in good spirits, and the day would be ours. And long after I laid down, he was going about among the soldiers, encouraging them, and telling them that the old wagoner (Morgan) would crack his whip over Ben (Tarleton) in the morning, as sure as they lived. "Just hold up your heads, boys, give them three fires, and you will be free. And then, when you return to your homes, how the old folks will bless you, and the girls will kiss you for your gallant conduct." About sun-rise the British advanced at a sort of trot, with a loud halloo; it was the most beautiful line I ever say. When they shouted, I heard Morgan say, "They give us the British halloo, boys - give them the Indian whoop;" and he galloped along the lines, cheering the men, and telling them not to fire until they could see the whites of their eyes. The militia fired first, they being in advance. At first, it was pop, pop, pop, and then a whole volley; but when the regulars fired, it seemed like one sheet of flame from right to left! Oh! it was beautiful! I heard old Colonel Fair say that John Savage fired the first gun in this battle.

After the second forming of the militia, the fight became general and unintermitting. In the

hottest of it, I saw Colonel Brandon coming at full speed to the rear, and waving his sword to Colonel Washington. In a moment, the order to charge was given. We made a most furious charge, and cutting through the British cavalry, we wheeled and charged them in the rear. In this charge, I exchanged my tackey for the finest horse I ever rode; it was the quickest swap I ever made in my life. At this moment, the bugle sounded: we made a half circuit at full speed, and came upon the rear of the British line, shouting and charging like madmen. At the same moment, Colonel Howard gave the order, "charge bayonet," and the day was ours - the British line broke - many of them laid down their arms and surrendered, while the rest took to the wagon road, and did their prettiest sort of running away. After this, Major Jolly and seven or eight of us resolved on an excursion to capture some of the baggage. We went about twelve miles, and captured two British soldiers, two negroes, and two horses laden with portmanteaus. One of the portmanteaus belonged to a paymaster in the British service, and contained gold. I rode along some miles with my prisoners and baggage towards our camp, when I met a party which I soon discovered to be British. I attempted to fly, but, my horse being stiff by the severe exercise I had given him, they overtook me. My pistol was empty, so I drew my sword and made battle; I never fought so hard in my life. In a few minutes, one finger on my left hand was split; then I received a cut on my sword arm. In the next instant a cut from a sabre across my forehead (the scar of which I shall carry to my grave); the skin slipped down over my eyes, and the blood blinded me. Then came a thrust in the right shoulder blade, then a cut upon the left shoulder, and a last cut, which you may feel for yourself on the back of my head, and I fell upon my horse's neck. They took me down, bound up my wounds, and replaced me on my horse, a prisoner of war.

damage on the British, who thought that their planned withdrawal past the left flank of the Continentals was the first sign of an American rout. The British therefore pressed forward right into the fire of the Continentals. Only then did Morgan unleash his double envelopment: the cavalry swept around onto the British right, and the re-formed militiamen onto their left. With his main force trapped and forced to surrender, Tarleton escaped with his small cavalry reserve. The Battle of Cowpens was a classic victory in which, for the loss of 73 casualties (12 killed and 61 wounded) the Americans killed 110 British and captured another 830.

Knowing that Cornwallis was not far away, Morgan moved with great speed to escape the British. In the next five days, he moved 100 miles. He crossed two rivers before he rejoined Greene, who had moved north from Cheraw Hill. The reunited Southern Army pulled back to the Dan River in southern Virginia with the British in pursuit. Cornwallis felt that this was the moment for a supreme effort. To allow his army to move faster, he ordered the destruction of all baggage, wagons, and surplus supplies. Greene kept his forces just in front of the British, swinging back from the unfordable Dan River into North Carolina during February and crossing the upper reaches of the Cape Fear River. During this stage of the campaign Greene lost the services of Morgan, who was forced by arthritis to quit.

On March 15, Greene halted on ground of his own choosing at Guilford Court House and offered battle. The Americans now numbered 4,500 men (1,500 Continentals and 3,000 militiamen) to 1,900 British regulars. The British fought with the utmost determination and, despite their smaller numbers, drove the militiamen off the field and finally gained the upper hand. Greene broke off the battle and retired in good order, leaving the British victorious. But the Battle of Guilford Court House was a Pyrrhic victory for the British: American losses were 78 dead and 183 wounded, while those of the British were 93 dead and 439 wounded. Having lost more than one-quarter of his force and virtually without supplies, Cornwallis had no option but to pull back,

The only non-American on the field during the Battle of Cowpens was the British commander, Lieutenant Colonel Sir Banastre Tarleton.

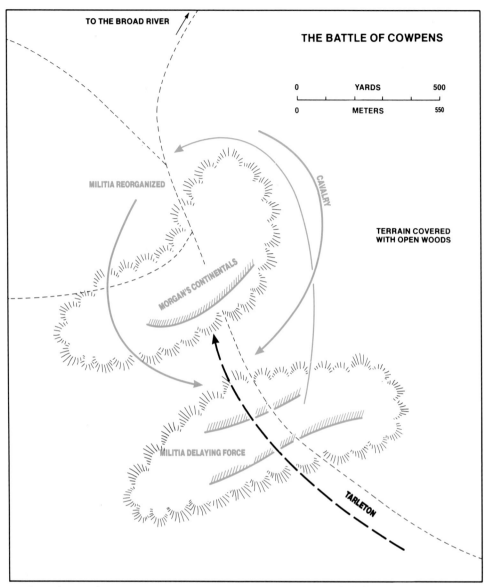

THE BATTLE OF COWPENS

TO THE BROAD RIVER

0   YARDS   500

0   METERS   550

MILITIA REORGANIZED

CAVALRY

TERRAIN COVERED WITH OPEN WOODS

MORGAN'S CONTINENTALS

MILITIA DELAYING FORCE

TARLETON

moving down the Cape Fear River to Wilmington. He decided that Georgia and South Carolina could no longer be held, and between April and May 1781, marched with his 1,500 men to join the expedition that Clinton had sent into Virginia.

Despite his tactical defeat at Guilford Court House, Greene knew that his army was in far better shape than it had been only six months earlier and responded rapidly to Cornwallis's withdrawal. The American commander followed Cornwallis most of the way to the Cape Fear River and turned off to the southwest to eliminate the British outposts in South Carolina with the support of the guerrilla units commanded by Marion, Pickens, and Sumter. The first British outpost to be tackled was that of Colonel Francis Rawdon at Camden, and in the Battle of Hobkirk's Hill on April 25, the American forces were firmly checked. One by one, the smaller British outposts fell to detachments of Greene's army or to guerrillas. There were however, other American reverses at Fort Ninety-Six and at Eutaw Springs. Fort Ninety-Six was taken under siege on May 22, but on June 19, a British force relieved the garrison, which fell back with the relief force to Charleston. On September 8, Greene's 2,400-man force attacked the 2,000-man British detachment commanded by Lieutenant Colonel

Left: Lieutenant Colonel Sir Banastre Tarleton was an infamous British leader in the southern campaign.

Below: The Battle of Eutaw Springs on September 8, 1781, was a British tactical victory, but the weakening of the overall British position meant that it was followed by a retreat to Charleston.

Alexander Stewart at Eutaw Springs. After an early success, he was driven back, but Stewart's losses were so heavy that he, too, was forced to retreat to Charleston.

Despite his losses and reverses at the tactical level, in which he had failed to win a single battle, Greene had achieved his strategic objective. By October 1781, the British had lost Georgia and South Carolina with the exception of their garrisons in the ports of Savannah and Charleston.

American Victory in Sight

The way was now set for American victory in the Revolutionary War, especially as the division between Clinton and Cornwallis was now as effective a hindrance to British efforts as the division between Howe and Burgoyne had been in 1777. Clinton was Cornwallis's superior, but Cornwallis had the ear of the government in London and thus felt himself able to conduct his operations without any real regard to Clinton's urgings. For this reason, Cornwallis felt that he was able to strike off into the interior of the Carolinas. Clinton had insisted that all operations should be conducted within reasonable distance of seaborne reinforcement and, by implication, evacuation. When Cornwallis eventually moved to Virginia, he did so without even notifying Clinton.

In 1779, Clinton started an effort to disrupt economic life in Virginia by raiding

Infantrymen of the Continental Army in 1779, with their uniforms set apart by state distinctions. By this time, the men of the Continental Army were a match for the men of the British and German infantry in most of the disciplines of formal warfare.

up its rivers. He knew that such raids would encourage local loyalists and might open the way for the establishment of a British base in the Chesapeake Bay region. This, Clinton hoped, could form one arm of the pincer movement with which he hoped to take Pennsylvania. The other arm would be provided by his currently inactive army in New York. An initial raid in the Hampton Roads area during 1779 had proved highly successful, but a second raid in 1780 had to be diverted to Charleston to provide Cornwallis with reinforcements after the King's Mountain setback. On December 30, 1780, a third raid arrived at Hampton Roads. Under the command of Arnold, this force of 1,600 men had orders to destroy American supplies, prevent the movement of reinforcements for Greene, and

American cavalry under the command of Henry Lee, better known as "Light Horse Harry," at the Battle of Guilford Court House on March 15, 1781. The battle was another British tactical success that was followed by strategic retreat, this time to Wilmington.

Major General Anthony Wayne was nicknamed ''Mad Anthony,'' but was one of the better American commanders in the closing stages of the Revolutionary War.

rally the loyalists. Arnold swept up the James River to seize Richmond on January 5, and after razing the city, he started back toward Portsmouth. Inconclusive operations against American forces commanded by von Steuben followed.

Virginian Coastal Operation

Arnold's presence in Virginia was a magnet to both sides. Washington's response was the dispatch of de Lafayette with 1,200 Continentals, and a plea to the French in Newport for a naval squadron to cut Arnold's seaborne lines of communication and ferry in a number of French troops. The plan was thrown into disarray by the First BAttle of the Delaware Capes on March 16. A British squadron of eight line of battle ships under Arbuthnot met Commodore Sochet Destouches's eight French line of battle ships: the British had three ships dismasted, but the French retired to Newport. Clinton sent in another 2,600 men under Major General William Phillips, who assumed command over all the British forces on his arrival.

The combined British expeditions then raided further along the Virginia coastal and James River regions before moving south to link up with Clinton's force advancing from Wilmington. Phillips died at Petersburg on May 10, but ten days later, the link-up of ten British forces put Cornwallis in command of Virginia operations, which could call on 8,000 men including the garrison of Portsmouth.

De Lafayette had arrived in Richmond on April 29 and took command of all American forces. This gave him a strength of 3,550 men, including his 1,200 veteran Continentals and von Steuben's largely inexperienced men. Further reinforcement was on its way from Washington in the form of Wayne's brigade of 800 Continentals, which joined de Lafayette on June 10. Between May and July, Cornwallis tried to bring the Americans to battle. But even with militia reinforcement, de

The Marquis de Lafayette leads his men against the British during one of the later campaigns of the Revolutionary War. De Lafayette showed great skill in engaging the British only when he had the advantage. Otherwise he slipped away to avoid battle and conserve his strength.

Lafayette was still considerably outnumbered and kept slipping away from the British, leading them around large portions of eastern Virginia.

Again, disagreement between the British generals played into the hands of the Americans. Cornwallis thought that Clinton's plan for a pincer offensive against Pennsylvania was militarily poor, while Clinton thought that Cornwallis's attempt to operate deep in Virginia would succeed no better than his operations deep in the Carolinas. Clinton finally gave Cornwallis a direct order to return to the coast, establish a base of operations, and return a part of the British force to New York. Reluctantly, Cornwallis headed for Portsmouth, with de Lafayette following closely. At Jamestown Ford on July 6, the British laid a neat ambush and caught Wayne's brigade. Although taken by surprise, the American veterans fought off the British assault and, despite heavy losses, counterattacked before retiring in good order. The British continued their retreat without further hindrance.

Cornwallis Bottles Himself Up at Yorktown

Cornwallis had been fighting Clinton's demand that part of the Virginia expedition should be returned to New York. On July 20, new orders from Clinton reached Cornwallis: no men need be returned to New York, and Cornwallis was to take and hold the tip of the Virginia peninsula at Yorktown, between the James and York Rivers. Cornwallis had concentrated most of his forces in Yorktown by August 4, giving him a strength of 7,000 men here and in a smaller garrison on the other side of the mouth of the York River estuary at Gloucester Point. De Lafayette had cautiously moved to a covering position with 4,500 men at nearby West Point, at the same time, informing Washington

Cornwallis surrendered at Yorktown on October 19, 1781.

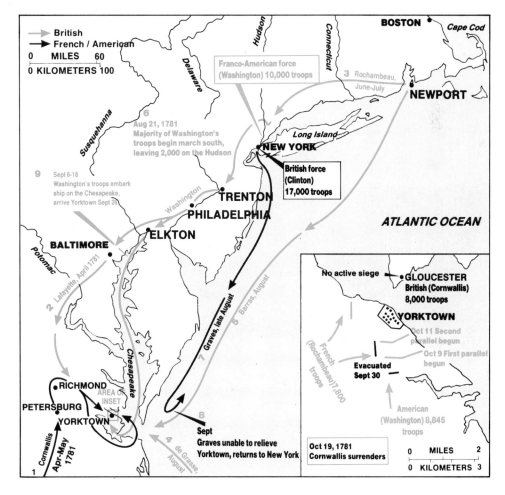

Major General William Heath was the American officer charged with creating the diversion in New York designed to persuade Clinton that the Franco-American allies were planning a northern effort in 1781.

of the latest British move.

Washington had meanwhile been trying to persuade de Rochambeau to commit his French troops to a combined Franco-American assault on Clinton in New York during the summer of 1781. On May 21, Washington and de Rochambeau met near New York to develop a common strategy. The two men agreed that, with British land strength concentrated in two places (New York and the Chesapeake Bay area), the allies' best hope for a victory was to use the growing French naval strength in the West Indies to cut the maritime line of communication between Clinton and Cornwallis. This would allow allied sea and land power to be concentrated against the weaker of the British

Captain, Continental Navy (1780)

As in the Royal Navy, captains of the Continental Navy seldom wore a complete regulation uniform, though a notable exception was Captain Abraham Whipple of Providence, Rhode Island. This officer is thought to have fired the first shot of the Revolutionary War at sea, and had already been involved in the *Gaspee* incident of 1772, when the British revenue cutter of that name ran aground off Narragansett and was burned by local people. Whipple's career ended in 1780, when he surrendered his entire squadron at the fall of Charleston. In March 1777, senior officers of the Continental Navy proposed a new uniform coat of blue lined in white with gold lacing and epaulets, but this was not officially recognized, even though some officers wore it. In 1781, the Continental Congress ordered that no officer was to wear ''any gold lace, embroidery or vellum, other than such as Congress of the Commander-in-Chief of the Army or Navy shall direct.''

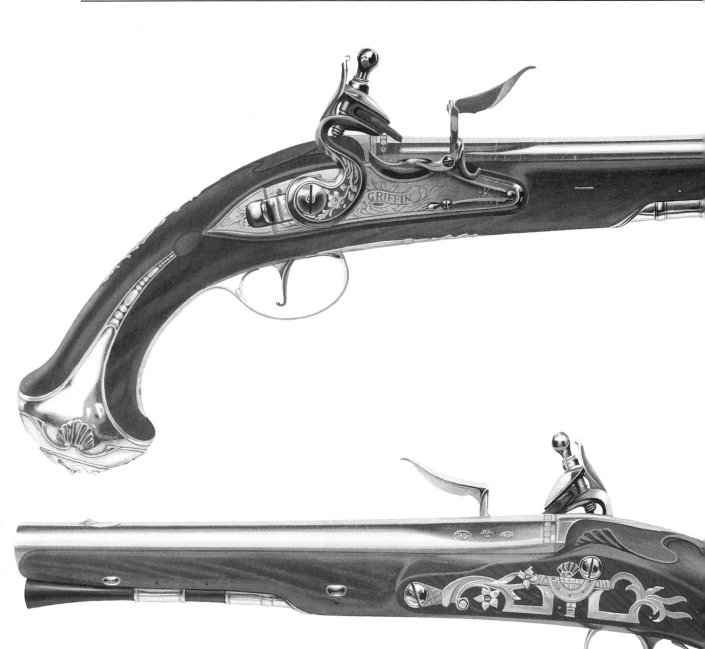

The matched flintlock
pistols carried by the
American
commander-in-chief
were a fine
pair made in London,
and a notably good
example of the
gunsmith's art in this
period.

enclaves. A French frigate was dispatched to the West Indies to deliver Washington's request to Admiral Francois-Joseph le Comte de Grasse. During June and July, de Rochambeau moved up from Newport with 4,000 men and put his French army under Washington's command. This gave the American commander-in-chief about 10,000 men, but his prospects were still uncertain as Clinton had at least 17,000 men in New York.

One day after de Grasse had sailed from the West Indies on August 13 with an additional 3,500 French troops collected from Haiti, Washington learned that the French admiral's destination was not to be New York, but Chesapeake Bay, where he should arrive later in the month and be able to stay until mid-October. Washington received this information just after de Lafayette's report about Cornwallis' retirement into the Yorktown peninsula. Here at last was the allies' chance to cut off and destroy a large segment of the British army in America. There was no unified command of inter-allied land and naval forces at the formal level, but in practice, cooperation was now good. Washington decided to move quickly. Admiral Louis le Comte de Barras sailed from Newport with his squadron to link up with de Grasse while de Lafayette was ordered to contain Cornwallis. Major General William Heath was left a force of 2,000 men with which to deceive Clinton that the allies were still planning an attack on New York. On August 21, Washington's combined Franco-American army started to march with the utmost speed and secrecy toward Virginia. The allied army had reached Virginia before Clinton realized that he had been deceived.

The Second Battle of the Delaware Capes

On August 30, de Grasse arrived in Chesapeake Bay with 24 ships of the line, and a few days later 3,500 French troops were disembarked to reinforce de

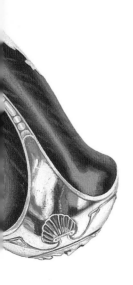

Right: Each side knew that an American victory at Yorktown in 1781 would decide the outcome of the Revolutionary War in favor of the United States. Here, Washington fires the first shot of the siege during October 3.

By an irony typical of history, the decisive battle of the Revolutionary War involved no Americans. The Second Battle of the Delaware Capes was fought on September 5, 1781, between British and French fleets. The tactical result was a tie that left the French in control of Chesapeake Bay when the British pulled back to New York, leaving Cornwallis to his fate in Yorktown.

Lafayette. Late in the month the British naval commander in New York, Admiral Thomas Graves, sailed with 19 ships of the line to intercept de Barras and prevent de Grasse's entry into Chesapeake Bay.

Failing to find de Barras, Graves made for Chesapeake Bay. On reaching Hampton Roads on September 5, he found that the French fleet had already entered the bay. De Grasse sortied against Graves in the

Second Battle of the Delaware Capes. The first eight French ships rounded Cape Henry well clear of the rest of the French fleet, but Graves failed to seize the opportunity this offered for piecemeal destruction of the French. The result was inconclusive. For the next four days, the two fleets maneuvered to secure the tactical advantage. This allowed de Barras to slip into Chesapeake Bay unmolested, and

The Franco-American land forces besieging Yorktown knew after the Second Battle of the Delaware Capes that a British defeat was now inevitable. Even so, they planned and executed their effort in the completely scientific manner of contemporary siege warfare.

de Grasse then retired into the bay. Graves then decided that he lacked the strength to force a passage into Chesapeake Bay, so he returned to New York.

This sealed the fate of Yorktown, and with it the British defeat in the Revolutionary War. On September 6, Washington's army reached Head of Elk. Between that day and September 18, they embarked in a flotilla of mainly French ships at Head of Elk, Baltimore and Annapolis for the journey down Chesapeake Bay and around the eastern tip of the Yorktown peninsula. They landed unopposed at Williamsburg, on the southwestern shore of the peninsula, on September 26. De Lafayette's men had meanwhile moved down the peninsula. By September 28, Yorktown had been completely surrounded.

Including some 3,000 Virginian militiamen, Washington had 8,845 American and 7,800 French troops under his command for the siege of 8,000

British. He sensibly left the conduct of the siege to experienced French engineers, who were excellently equipped and could also call on the service of some of France's latest artillery. In a move that greatly aided the allies, Cornwallis abandoned his forward position on September 30, and by October 6, the engineers started digging their first trench 600 yards in front of the British main positions. Three days later, the allied artillery began its bombardment from this trench. On October 11, the engineers had pushed forward about 200 yards of the zigzag trench that extended toward the British position and allowed the start of work on the second trench line. On October 14, American and French infantry stormed two British redoubts that allowed the siege works to be extended to the edge of the York River. On October 16, a major British counterattack was beaten back. Cornwallis now saw that he could not hold Yorktown. He tried to

Washington inspects French artillery in the trenches around Yorktown. The allies used 52 guns to shell the British garrison without respite, and the storming of two British redoubts on October 14 ended all chance that the besieged army might be able to slip away.

evacuate part of his force across the York River to Point Gloucester, where the British beachhead was contained by only small American forces. But a storm prevented the execution of this plan on October 16, and Cornwallis realized that his only hope was relief from New York.

British Surrender at Yorktown

Clinton too had come to this conclusion, but the decision to send Graves with a reinforced fleet and 7,000 troops had taken so long that the fleet did not sail until October 17, the day on which Cornwallis opened surrender negotiations with Washington. The American commander-in-chief allowed two days for written proposals to be prepared, but demanded complete surrender by Cornwallis. On October 19, the British garrison of Yorktown marched out and

laid down its arms. On October 24, Graves's fleet arrived with Clinton and his 7,000-man reinforcement, but seeing that the Yorktown garrison had already surrendered it returned to New York. Washington tried to persuade de Grasse to support attacks on the British bases at Charleston and Wilmington, but the French admiral decided that the dangers of the storm season were too great for any further delay. The French sailed for the West Indies.

The American and French victory at Yorktown effectively put an end to the War. When news of the defeat reached London, the government fell, to be replaced by a more realistic administration that decided to end hostilities. More than two years were to pass before the provisions of the Treaty of Paris were implemented and the British completed their evacuation. With the war effectively won, later land operations were undertaken on

GLORIOUS NEWS.

PROVIDĒCE, October 25, 1781.

Three o'Clock, P. M.

THIS MOMENT an EXPRESS arrived at his Honour the Deputy-Governor's, from Col. Chriſtopher Olney, Commandant on Rhode-Iſland, announcing the important Intelligence of the Surrender of Lord Cornwallis and his Army, an Account of which was printed This Morning at Newport, and is as follows, viz.

Newport, October 25, 1781.

YESTERDAY afternoon arrived in this Harbour Capt. Lovett, of the Schooner Adventure, from York-River, in Chefapeak-Bay (which he left the 20th Inſtant) and brought us the glorious News of the Surrender of Lord CORNWALLIS and his Army Priſoners of War to the allied Army, under the Command of our illuſtrious General, and the French Fleet, under the Command of his Excellency the Count de GRASSE.

A Ceſſation of Arms took Place on Thurſday the 18th Inſtant, in Conſequence of Propoſals from Lord Cornwallis for a Capitulation. His Lordſhip propoſed a Ceſſation of Twenty-four Hours, but Two only were granted by His Excellency General WASHINGTON. The Articles were completed the ſame Day, and the next Day the allied Army took Poſſeſſion of York-Town.

By this glorious Conqueſt, NINE THOUSAND of the Enemy, including Seamen, fell into our Hands, with an immenſe Quantity of Warlike Stores, a forty Gun Ship, a Frigate, an armed Veſſel, and about One Hundred Sail of Tranſports.

Above: Cornwallis surrenders to Washington at Yorktown. Surrender negotiations began on October 17, the day that a relief force sailed from New York. On October 19, the British garrison marched out to lay down its arms and effectively ended the Revolutionary War.
Left: Typical of the news broadsheets that confirmed the events at Yorktown for the American people was this example, published in Providence, Rhode Island, on October 25.
Opposite: A. M. Willard's painting "The Spirit of '76" (perhaps better known as "Yankee Doodle") summarizes the patriotism of the Revolutionary War for many people.

only a small scale. In November 1781, Washington marched his men back to the blockade of New York and established his headquarters at Newburgh. De Rochambeau wintered with his forces in Virginia before returning to Rhode Island in the fall of 1782 en route to Boston, where the French army embarked and set sail for France on December 24. The only fighting of the period was the skirmishing around Charleston, where Greene was maintaining his blockade of the British base. Despite the fact that the British had clearly lost the war, the loyalists did not want to abandon the struggle. There were a number of border raids of a particularly bloody nature. Typical was the August 1782 raid from Quebec by loyalists and Indian supporters under the command of an American traitor, Simon Girty. With about 240 men Girty pushed across the Ohio River into what is now Kentucky attacking Bryan's Station on August 15. Driven back here, the raiders prepared an ambush of the type feared by Colonel

Left: Captain John Barry, commander of the frigate U.S.S. *Alliance* that completed a successful cruise in 1781.

Right: Engraved after George W.Maynard's commemorative painting entitled simply ''76,'' this illustration again reveals the simple nobility with which the Revolutionary War has been characterized by later generations.

Daniel Boone and sprang it on the pursuing force at Blue Licks on August 19 before escaping to safety.

The year 1781 marked the high point in American privateer operations against the British, but the only regular naval action undertaken in this year by the Americans was the cruise of the U.S.S. *Alliance*, a frigate commanded by Captain John Barry. The American warship sailed to France and back, and on the return journey it captured two British sloops, H.M.S.

Atlanta and H.M.S *Trepassy*, and also took a pair of British privateers.

Formal Independence for the United States

A new British government was formed on March 20, 1782, which began negotiations for peace on April 9. In New York, Sir Guy Carleton took over from Clinton, and

Below: Washington and his officers at the commander's farewell dinner, held in Fraunces' Tavern on the corner of Pearl and Broad Streets in New York, on December 4, 1783.
Right: Washington resigns as American commander-in-chief on December 23, 1783. Appearing before the Continental Congress in a session in Annapolis, Washington said: "...I retire from the great theater of Action; and bidding an Affectionate farewell to this August body under whose orders I have so long acted, I here offer my Commission and take my leave of all the employments of public life."

the work of evacuating all British troops to New York continued. Wilmington had been evacuated in January, Savannah was cleared on July 11, and troops left Charleston on December 14. On November 30, the Treaty of Paris was signed, to become effective on the conclusion of British hostilities with France and Spain in the Mediterranean, the West Indies, and off

the coast of India. The treaty recognized the independence of the United States and ended Great Britain's war with the new country. The Continental Congress ratified the treaty on April 15, and rapid demobilization of the Continental Army followed in June. Starting on November 23, the British evacuated New York, their last American toehold. On December 4, the day on which the last British transport sailed from New York, Washington said farewell to his officers at Fraunces' Tavern. On December 23, 1783, Washington formally resigned his commission at a special Congressional session and retired to private life. The Revolutionary War was finally over, and the United States was a nation with no foreign troops on its soil.

Glossary

Adjutant general Commanding officer responsible for manpower.

Ammunition Propellant (gunpowder) and projectiles for artillery and small arms.

Artillery Guns too large and heavy for use by a single person, and therefore mounted on a wheeled carriage and served by a crew of several men.

Battalion Tactical unit made up of several companies.

Battery Artillery equivalent of an infantry company.

Bayonet Sword-like blade attached to the muzzle of a musket or rifle for use in close-quarter combat.

Brigade Tactical grouping containing several battalions.

Cavalry Troops who fight on horseback.

Chain of command Sequence of commanding officers from highest to lowest, through which command is exercised.

Commissary general Commanding officer responsible for food.

Company Basic sub-component of a battalion, in 1776 a figure of 91 men was established as the size of a company.

Court martial Court for the trial of people subject to military law.

Division Tactical grouping of two or more brigades, often provided with support elements so that it can exist and fight by itself.

Earthwork Defensive geographical feature created by excavating and mounding dirt.

Enlistment Length of time for which a soldier agrees to serve in the army.

Firepower Overall term for a unit's total weapon strength.

Flank Extreme left or right of the body of soldiers in any one position.

Flotilla Fleet of boats or small ships.

Frigate Warship with less than 60 guns, designed for raiding and reconnaissance rather than involvement in fleet actions.

Front Lateral length of a body of soldiers between their two flanks.

Garrison Body of soldiers assigned to a base or area of operations mainly for defense.

Infantry Foot soldiers.

Inspector general Commanding officer responsible for training.

Light infantry Foot soldiers used for reconnaissance and skirmishing, and therefore more lightly equipped than regular infantry.

Line of communication The main route over which supplies (food and ammunition), commands, reinforcements, etc., pass to the front.

Militia Units of able-bodied men provided by a colony or state for short-term service.

Minuteman Able-bodied person prepared to turn out at a minute's notice in times of emergency.

Musket Eighteenth-century weapon: a smooth-bore weapon firing its ball without the spin imparted by a rifle.

Parallel A trench dug parallel to a defensive feature to provide cover for assaulting soldiers. Parallels were gradually pushed closer to the objective by digging zigzag trenches in the direction of the objective and then digging lateral trenches to make a new parallel at the forward end of the zigzag "sap."

Privateer Civilian ship with a license from its national authorities which was used for raiding merchant shipping.

Quartermaster general Commanding officer responsible for supply of all goods, armaments, material, etc.

Rearguard Rearmost element of a fighting force, designed to protect the rear during an advance, and to check the enemy during a retreat.

Reconnaissance Mission by a small group of soldiers to obtain information about the enemy's position, strength, and movements.

Redoubt Outwork of a defensive system, usually lacking flanking defenses.

Regiment Tactical unit composed of two or more battalions.

Regular soldier Full-time soldier as opposed to part-time militiaman.

Rifle Infantry weapon which fires its ball with a stabilizing spin for greater accuracy and range.

Ship of the line Warship with more than 60 guns, designed to fight in fleet actions.

Siege Scientifically planned and executed capture of an enemy position by cutting it off and then gradually closing in before delivering the final assault.

Small arms General term for weapons operated by one person.

Strategy Art of fighting a war or campaign.

Tactics Art of fighting a battle.

Volley Hail of fire delivered when many small arms are discharged at the same moment.

Bibliography

Balderston, Marion and David Syrett (ed.). *The Lost War: Letters from British Officers During the American Revolution.*
(Horizon Press, New York, 1975).
First-hand views from the other side.

Boatner, Mark M., III *Encyclopedia of the American Revolution.*
(David McKay Co., New York, 1974).
Outstanding alphabetical coverage of all aspects of the war.

Busch, Noel F. *Winter Quarters.*
(Mentor, New York, 1974). Winter at Valley Forge.

Carrington, Henry B. *Battles of the American Revolution.*
(A. S. Barnes & Co., New York, 1877).

Coggins, Jack. *Ships and Seamen of the American Revolution.*
(Stackpole Books, Harrisburg, PA, 1969).
Good details on the construction and handling of ships in the age of sail.

Cuneo, John R. *The Battles of Saratoga.*
(Macmillan, New York, 1967).
The decisive battle, part of a battle series aimed at younger readers.

Davis, Burke, *The Campaign That Won America.*
(Dial Press, New York, 1970).
A more sophisticated account of the Saratoga campaign.

Davis, Burke. *The Cowpens-Guildford Courthouse Campaign.*
(J. B. Lippincott Co., New York, 1962).
Good popular history of the duel of wits between Cornwallis and Greene.

Esposito, Vincent J. (ed.). *The West Point Atlas of American Wars 1689-1900.*
(Frederick A. Praeger, New York, 1959).
A fine map book coordinated with easy-to-understand text.

Fleming, Thomas J. *Beat the Last Drum: The Siege of Yorktown 1781.*
(St. Martins Press, New York, 1963).
The origins of the American way of war.

Ketchum, Richard M. (ed.). *The American Heritage Book of the Revolution.*
(American Heritage Publishing Co., New York, 1971).
A lavishly illustrated, fine popular history.

Ketchum, Richard M. *The Winter Soldiers.*
(Doubleday & Co., Garden City, NY, 1973).
Washington's early campaigns showing him to be truly the 'indispensible man.'

Lancaster, Bruce. *From Lexington to Liberty.*
(Doubleday & Co., Garden City, NY, 1955).

Lossing, Benton J. *Pictorial Field-Book of the Revolution.*
(Harper & Brothers, New York, 1852).
Full of good terrain sketches and human interest stories by someone who visited the sites while they remained nearly unchanged from the war days.

Lumpkin, Henry. *From Savannah to Yorktown.*
(Paragon House, New York, 1981).
The war in the south.

Matthews, William and Dixon Wecter. *Our Soldiers Speak, 1775-1918.*
(Little Brown & Co., Boston, 1943).
First-hand accounts.

Miller, Nathan. *Sea of Glory.*
(David McKay Co., New York, 1974).
The Continental Navy.

Rankin, Hugh F. *Francis Marion: The Swamp Fox.*
(Thomas Y. Crowell Co., New York, 1873)
The war's most famous guerrilla leader.

Roberts, Kenneth. *The Battle of Cowpens.*
(Doubleday Co., Garden City, NY, 1958).
Morgan's masterpiece in easy-to-read detail.

Scheer, George F. and Hugh F. Rankin. *Rebels & Redcoats.*
(World Publishing Co., New York, 1957).

Wheeler, Richard. *Voices of 1776.*
(Thomas Y. Crowell Co., New York, 1972).
Eyewitness accounts of the American Revolution.

Index

Page numbers in *italics* refer to illustration.